The Church
in Ruins

The Church in Ruins

Brief Thoughts on II Timothy, Paul's Last Letter to the Church

Clyde L. Pilkington, Jr.

BIBLE STUDENT'S PRESS™
Windber, Pennsylvania

The Church in Ruins – *Brief Thoughts on II Timothy, Paul's Last Letter to the Church*
by Clyde L. Pilkington, Jr.
Copyright © 2009 by Clyde L. Pilkington, Jr.
All rights reserved.

Originally published in the *Bible Student's Notebook* (ISSN: 1936-936) © 2001

Executive Editor: André Sneidar
Layout and Design: Great Adventure in Faith

Cover design by Clyde L. Pilkington, III
Cover photography by Aaron Locker (ruins of Ephesus)

ISBN-10:   1-934251-59-3
ISBN-13:   978-1-934251-59-1

Published by:
Bible Student's Press™
An imprint of *Pilkington & Sons*
P.O. Box 265
Windber, PA 15963
1-800-784-6010

For information on *Bible Student's Press*™ releases, visit
   www.BibleStudentsPress.com

For information on other Bible study resources, visit
   www.StudyShelf.com

Printed in the United States of America.

Dedicated to …

The members of Christ's Body who, over the past two millennia, have, in spite of opposition and trial, faithfully carried out their ambassadorship, outside of the religious system.

PREFACE

The truths that we learn are designed to change our lives. As we study God's Word we should grow; and as we grow there comes a point in our lives where we are moved to make decisions. These times are crucial to our continued spiritual growth.

The truths presented in this book were borne out of a deep, long, heartfelt struggle. While a pastor I began to question the legitimacy of the human organization called "church," including my own role in this man-made system.

I eventually walked away from "professional" ministry and institutional Christianity. This was not an easy process – it was gut wrenching, in fact. All I had known about the Christian walk was rooted in them. For the next few years I was severely tried, with continual pressure from without and from within always present with me to return to the organized religious system that I had left.

I longed intensely for spiritual direction and personal peace. In the quietness of my own wilderness journey, I found it in the study of II Timothy. The truths of this epistle would become vibrantly alive to me and would clearly point out the way on this new course of my life, as they had to the dear saints who had walked this pathway before me.

This work is a brief and feeble attempt at presenting the truths of II Timothy as I have come to embrace them. It is not a call for a re-awakening of "the church," because it is apparent that this is not Father's plan. Rather, it is a call to individual men – men whose place in the "Christian" religious system has left them empty, stagnant and restless – to awaken to Father's call to be His faithful servant and stand outside of that system to look for other faithful men as well.

It is my prayer that the reader of this book is one of those faithful men whom Father is calling; and that these few pages will be used of Him to help you on your journey in the same measure that it has helped me in mine.

For the love of God, and His truth,

Clyde

Your fellow,
Clyde L. Pilkington, Jr.

WHAT OTHERS HAVE SAID
ABOUT THIS BOOK

What a thrill to know that I'm not crazy after all! – *PA*

This stuff is so much where we're at. – *NC*

This is one powerful message! I don't care what others may say, you are right on the money. Press on. – *HI*

I have come face to face with "the church" being a hindrance to the spiritual growth of my own family as I have always put "the church" first. I have since resigned my position in "the church" and there have been positive changes in my family. Thank you for the hours and hours of study you put into teaching those like myself who still have so much to learn. – *IL*

Much of what you have said I have seen on my own, but needed to see it in writing. ... I thank God for you and your steadfast adherence to the truth, you are a very great help to those of us who are in the thick of it. Keep on keeping on; we need your leadership and encouragement as the battle continues. – *FL*

Great clarification on the subject. – *WI*

Thank God that you are putting these things in their contexts ... This is groundbreaking stuff. – *OH*

I appreciate your bold stand for the truth. – *NC*

We know you must be getting a lot of flack. Don't let it get to you, you're telling the truth. – *MI*

Indeed the institutionalization and compartmentalization of Christianity in our culture has been used by Satan to take captive God's people. – *CA*

Impressive summarization of the state of affairs within Christianity ... Thanks for your teaching; it makes me hungry. – *TX*

It is good to know that some "nuts" are screwed onto the right bolt! – *WI*

I know that you will receive much criticism … But your approach is truthful and loving. – *IL*

I want you to know what an encouragement you are to me and my family. I have had the same understanding of the church for some time now, but your statements about saints who are involved in religious systems opposing who they are in Christ was a real eye opener. – *MI*

Of all I read I am most impressed by your admission that you have changed from previous beliefs, thereby allowing for growth. – *OH*

I have learned many things from these studies. – *Philippines*

We appreciate the clarity of your understanding of the Scriptures. – *IL*

How can people dare argue with what the Bible plainly declares? – *IN*

I am now "outside the camp" with you. Thank you again for the encouragement to remain focused on the Word of God. We really know nothing of "church life" apart from God's revelation. The rest is chaff. – *IL*

EXCELLENT. Another nail driven by the TRUTH! – *WI*

It is a great happiness to me to see these insights on the Church … God be thanked that His Word is still here standing true for those who will study, meditate and pray in it. – *VA*

I know you have probably had some criticism, but I hope that it hasn't left you in despair … It takes real love for the Lord to stand unashamed for the truth of God's Word, and what He's doing today. … The members of the body of Christ should always be ready to adjust their thinking and way of life as they get new light. Keep up the good work. – *MI*

Priceless. No doubt, Clyde, you will suffer more persecution for this Timothy series. I hope so; you're really "racking up points" for your celestial allotment. We know that all this has been graciously granted to you. – *OH*

I have always wondered about some of these things. (But I never wanted to think about them too long!) I have felt alone for quite some time, because I did not "go to church." This is just another part of the mystery that most do not see, and once you do (just like the other truths of the mystery) you feel a peace that you didn't even know about. – *VA*

Having read this subject matter, I believe you have presented the whole truth. – *AZ*

Very helpful. This should make us think about where Christianity is at today. If the turning away from Paul's message happened so rapidly in Paul's day, we shouldn't expect to find much of it left in organized religion. – *South Africa*

These studies are laden with meaning. Every paragraph, every line, every word. And there seems to be new revelation in it for me. I think God is giving you to see into the marrow of this church deception. Thank you for writing this. – *OH*

Awesome. I've learned a lot from the Scriptures you've taught that I didn't understand before. I can look around and see the apostasy but I relax that God has everything lined up according to His purpose. Thanks for your teaching. – *TX*

CONTENTS

And the things that you have heard of me among many witnesses, the same commit to faithful men, who shall be able to teach others also.

~ II Timothy 2:2

INTRODUCTION

When people learn the truth about Paul's apostleship and message, they often ask questions like: "What happened to Christianity?" "When did the church abandon Paul's gospel?" "How did we get into such a mess?"

The real answer to these questions is not to be found in church history. The answer is found much earlier than that – in the writings of Paul, our Apostle.

Where does the believer who follows God fit in today's religions? To which denomination or church should we belong? In this book we will look at our Apostle's last words as found in the book of II Timothy. It is here that we will find the final marching orders for the church. Understanding this letter of Paul is essential to knowing how to walk as

> *A vessel unto honor, sanctified, and meet* [useful, profitable] *for the Master's use, and prepared unto every good work* (II Timothy 2:21).

Members of Christ's Body, "the Church" – the *ecclesia* – are God's called out ones. II Timothy is their true story.

Background

PAUL'S LOVING LETTER TO THE OUTSIDERS

Since the final days of Paul's ministry *the church,* the Body of Christ, has been in a state (not standing) of ruins. The history of its state has mirrored the account of Israel's apostasy. Israel never fully lived in all of the promises and position that the Lord had given to them. At one point they were even carried away from their divine calling into Babylonian captivity. When they were given the opportunity to return to their God-appointed land, only a small remnant even chose to leave the comforts and familiarity of Babylon and go back home.

So it is with *the church.* As a whole, its history is that of having long abandoned its position *in Christ.* In fact, the Body of Christ at large has remained satisfied and content in a similar "Babylonian captivity." Those who have been enlightened to their condition of captivity and their true identity and freedom in Christ, and have taken the journey out of "Babylon," have been but a few. So when we lament "poor Israel" and their long and sad story of apostasy, we need to take a prolonged look in the mirror and realize that the Body of Christ has done no better!

Paul testifies to this state of ruin in the book of II Timothy. He states straightforwardly that, *"all they which are in Asia are turned away from me"* (1:15). Now, what is so significant about this disclosure is that Ephesus (which was the capital city of the Roman province of Asia) is where Paul spent a two-year teaching ministry, the result of which was that, *"all they which dwelt in Asia heard the Word of the Lord Jesus"* (Acts 19:10). Quite a contrast of *alls,* is it not? It started with *"all ... heard"* and ended with *"all ... turned away."*

During the time between those two passages, Paul had even written an epistle to the Ephesian saints. This letter was one in which Paul laid forth the pinnacle of *"the revelation of the mystery"* that had been committed to his trust.

Yet these very saints, who had been benefactors of such a long personal ministry of Paul, and of such a rich epistle, *"ALL ... turned away"* from him. The Body of Christ lay in ruins as Paul lay in a Roman prison about to be executed.

PAUL'S MINISTRY IN ASIA

To grasp the significance of Paul's statement that, *"all they which are in Asia are turned away from me"* (1:15), we must first understand the meaning of "Asia."

"Asia" was a Roman province of Bible times that covered the western portion of the Asia Minor peninsula. The city of Ephesus was its capital. Paul dedicated a significant portion of his ministry to this region:

Asian Location	Acts Reference
Mysia	16:7
Troas	16:8
Ephesus	18:18-21; 19:1-41
Assos	20:13
Mitylene	20:14
Chios	20:15
Samos	20:15
Trogyllium	20:15
Miletus	20:15
Coos	21:1
Rhodes	21:1

… From the first day that I came into Asia … that by the space of three years I ceased not to warn every one night and day with tears … (Acts 20:18, 31).

A Serious Condition that Was Not Limited to Asia

This ruined condition of *the church,* the Body of Christ, was not limited to the Roman province of Asia. Paul addresses the Asian problem because this was where the recipient of his letter was. This is the ruins of which Timothy himself was aware. That's why he starts that statement, ***"This you know,*** that all they which *are in Asia are turned away from me."* Frankly, this apostasy of the Body of Christ proliferated throughout the Roman Empire.

Paul said, concerning his first trial date of this final Roman imprisonment, that *"no man stood with me, but all men forsook me"* (II Timothy 4:16). There was not one man in Rome who came and stood with Paul! This was after some 22 years of ministry in the Roman Empire. It was after writing a glorious letter to the saints at Rome, and after coming to Rome and having taught from his home there for two years.

> *And Paul dwelt two whole years in his own hired house, and received all who came in unto him, preaching the kingdom of God, and teaching those things which concern the Lord Jesus Christ, with all confidence, no man forbidding him* (Acts 28:30-31).

What happened to all the Roman saints? They ALL forsook him!

When folks inquire, as they often will, concerning when the problems of *the church* began, one need not look to various periods of human church history; one needs only to see the divine record of this apostasy as recorded in the book of II Timothy. As Paul was awaiting his execution in the dark, damp dungeon of Rome's prison, *the church,* the Body of Christ, lay in its own prison – a prison of apostasy and ruin!

THE WARNING TO THE ELDERS

Upon leaving the region of Asia, Paul warned the Ephesian elders (Acts 20:17-38; A.D. 60) of the serious dangers that lie ahead of them.

> *For I know this, that after my departing shall grievous wolves enter in among you, not sparing the flock. Also of your own selves shall men arise, speaking perverse things, to draw away disciples after them* (Acts 20:29-30).

Paul did not say, "There is a good chance, that after my departing ..." He said, *"For I **know** this ..."* Paul prophesied concerning the future of the Asian saints. The Body of Christ would not be spared this severe test; but would they heed this serious warning?

The Warning by His Epistles

That's not all!

After leaving, Paul also wrote three epistles to the saints in these provinces of Asia:

Ephesus (A.D. 64)
Colosse (A.D. 64)
Philemon (who resided in Colosse; A.D. 64)

Paul warned the Colossian saints of the real danger of being spoils of a spiritual war:

> *Beware lest any man spoil you ... you are complete in Him ...* (Colossians 2:8, 10).

> *Let no man therefore judge you ... Let no man beguile you ... not holding the Head* (Colossians 2:16-19).

Paul warned the Ephesian saints to be prepared for *"the evil day"* of testing that lay ahead.

> *Finally, my brothers, be strong in the Lord, and in the power of His might. Put on the whole armor of God, that you may be able to stand against the wiles of the devil. For we wrestle not against flesh and blood, but against principalities, against powers, against the rulers of the darkness of this world, against spiritual wickedness in high places. Wherefore take unto you the whole armor of God, that you may be able to withstand **in the evil day,** having done all to stand ...* (Ephesians 6:10-13).

Nevertheless, in less than a six-year span from the time he warned the Ephesian elders of these dangers, all those in Asia had turned away from Paul and his message (II Timothy 1:15).

What does Paul say would be the ultimate result of the Asian saints turning away from him?

> *For the time will come when they will not endure sound doctrine; but after their own lusts shall they heap to themselves teachers, having itching ears; and shall turn away their ears from the truth, and shall be turned unto fables* (II Timothy 4:3-4).

Just where does Asia – this region in which Paul invested so much – stand spiritually today? It is in the western portion of Turkey and is 98% Moslem! It does not pay to neglect the writings of Paul!

OUR APOSTLE'S LAST WORD

The book of II Timothy is of great significance because it is Paul's last epistle. It was written to detail the apostasy that was already upon *the church*. We benefit greatly from this letter when we realize this and take special note of its personal and individual nature. Paul's last word is not to *the church* as a whole, but to an *individual member* of it. It is a letter of edification and instruction in light of widespread apostasy.

II Timothy is one of Paul's "Prison Epistles," as can be noted in 1:8, 16-17. It was written during his second Roman imprisonment (around A.D. 67-68). As he wrote this letter to his closest friend, the time of his execution drew very near (4:16).

We take a little space to note what others have written regarding this crucial letter of II Timothy.

Sir Robert Anderson:

The same apostle who had exalted in the fact that, *"all they which dwelt in Asia heard the word of the Lord Jesus"* (Acts 19:10), lived to pen the sad lament, *"This thou knowest, that all they which are in Asia be turned away from me"* (II Timothy 1:15). And then, taking a still wider view of the condition of the church, he indicted the solemn forecast, *"But evil men and seducers shall wax worse and worse, deceiving and being deceived"* (II Timothy 3:13).[1]

C.I. Scofield:

Second Timothy has to do with the personal walk and testimony of a true servant of Christ in a day of apostasy and declension. The key phrases are, *"All they which are in Asia be turned away from me"* (1:15); and, *"A good soldier of Jesus Christ"* (2:3)[2]

1. Sir Robert Anderson, *The Buddha of Christendom,* page 37.
2. C.I. Scofield, the *Scofield Reference Bible.*

George Williams:

[II Timothy] views the Church in ruins, and instructs the man of God as to his personal conduct in the midst of the ruin"[3]

Charles Welch:

Instead of a church governed by bishops we have insistence upon individual witness. Consequently, while we value the earlier epistles of the mystery for the revelation that they bring, we value II Timothy rather for a message which fits the sad, apostate days in which our lot is cast.[4]

F.B. Hole:

We have no certain knowledge of how many years elapsed between the writing of the 1st and 2nd epistles to Timothy but evidently there had been sufficient time for the development of a big down-grade movement in the church of God. The diverse characters stamped upon the two epistles make this quite plain. In the first epistle Timothy is instructed as to good order in the church and exhorted to maintain it in the presence of disorder that threatened it. In the second we find serious defection has developed ... consequently that which is official is not mentioned and the appeal is to individual faithfulness.[5]

J.N. Darby:

The first of Timothy gives directions for the order of the assembly; the second, for the path of the servant of God when it is in disorder and failure ... The Second Epistle to Timothy has a very peculiar character ... Paul sees for himself the ruin of that which he had built and watched over so faithfully ... The principle therefore of individual faithfulness, of individual

---

3. George Williams, the *Student's Commentary on the Holy Scriptures*.
4. Charles Welch, *The Berean Expositor XXXI*.
5. F.B. Hole, *Paul's Epistles*.

responsibility to God, is established, and set above all other considerations.[6]

D.L. McCroskey:

When Paul was about to board his ship in Acts 20:37, his beloved Ephesian brethren *"wept sore"* and kissed him, sorrowing that *"they should see his face no more."* But in the Epistle before us, we see him some six years later writing that the time of his departure from this life is at hand. And this time, there are no brethren to weep and embrace him, and comfort him. *"Only Luke is with me,"* he wrote.

How tragic that the great world apostasy was already beginning, even before Paul's death ... They turned away from Paul and his message ... and Judaism and Christianity become more and more mixed together. Ever since, preachers in Christendom have shied away from Paul – even to this day! ...

Practically all error in Christendom today stems from ignorance or denial of Paul's gospel of grace and his revelation of the mystery. In Romans 16:25 he wrote *"Now to Him that is of power to stablish you according to my gospel, and the preaching of Jesus Christ, according to the revelation of the mystery, which was kept secret since the world began."* How, then, can believers be established in truth when they deny Paul's special gospel (Galatians 1:11-12), and the revelation of the mystery as revealed through him?[7]

E.W. Bullinger:

The prominent feature of this Epistle is the "church's" departure from the truth (see 1:16; 2:17; 3:8; 4:4). When *"all they which are in Asia (c.f. Acts 19:10) be turned away from"*

---

6. J.N. Darby, *The Synopsis of the Books of the Bible.*
7. D.L. McCroskey, *II Timothy – The Divine Outline of World Apostasy*, The Last Day Messenger, November-December, 1975.

Paul, he exhorts Timothy, his *"son,"* therefore to *"be strong in the grace that is in Christ Jesus."* No more is there heard, as in the First Epistle and in that to Titus, the apostolic guidance for church rule or administration of any kind. Only two things are possible now: *"Preach the word"* (4:2), and *"The things that thou hast heard of me among many witnesses, the same commit thou to faithful men, who shall be able to teach others also"* (2:2). ... Paul tells of even worse days to come, perilous, or grievous, times *"in the last days"* (3:1; 4:8), the only charge in connection with which is *"Continue thou in the things which thou hast learned and hast been assured of"* (3:14).[8]

A.E. Knoch:

[Paul] has the highest titles which a servant of Christ can obtain in this era. He has a triple crown, far more magnificent than that of the Roman pontiff today. He was a Herald, an Apostle and a Teacher of the nations. His parish was the world, including every nation on the inhabited earth. In time, his ministry extends throughout this era, for he did not only speak, but made his message immortal by his pen. He was the first to herald the abolition of death and to bring to light life and incorruption. None of the apostles before him had such a message. None had the scope of his, either in space or time. His teaching far transcends that of any other either before or after him ...

What was his earthly reward? Did they build him a vast cathedral, such as was later erected to honor Peter in Rome? Did they seat him on a jeweled throne with a glittering crown upon his head? Did they come to adore and kiss him as they now kiss "Saint" Peter's brazen toe? Far from all this! When our Lord was crucified, His disciples left Him and fled. So also, when Paul was imprisoned, most of his followers forsook him and were ashamed to have anything to do with him. Indeed, he was so cut off from his erstwhile friends that

---

8. E.W. Bullinger, *The Companion Bible*, p. 1808.

it was hard to find him, even by those who were not ashamed of him (II Timothy 1:17).

Why was Paul suffering these shameful indignities? Because he was God's ambassador to a rebellious world. Because, as the herald and apostle and teacher of the nations he was *faithful* to the evangel ["*gospel*"] committed to him. Because he made God's purpose known, and the grace which is ours in Christ Jesus through His crucifixion and burial and ascension and glorification. Because he taught the abolition of death and the vivification of all in his evangel. Because this shameful treatment of God's most highly honored and supremely blest [*sic*] of all the servants of Christ is essential as a background for the revelation of His transcendent grace, not only to mankind, but to all His creatures in the celestial spheres as well, not only now, but in the eons that impend.

Paul himself knew this; therefore he insists that he is not ashamed (II Timothy 1:12). However, he was not concerned so much about himself as about the evangel which had been committed to him. What would become of it after he was gone? Timothy, indeed, was left, and a few others; but the great bulk of those whom he had reached seem to have forsaken him. Moreover, there were forces at work which turned the saints from him and his teaching. Phygellus and Hermogenes were but samples of the many in the province of Asia, where he had reached such numbers, and to whom he had sent his grandest epistles. Yet he was not ashamed, because he knew Whom he had believed, and was persuaded that He is able to guard what was committed to him for that day (II Timothy 1:12).

One of the greatest miracles of the so-called "Christian centuries" is the continual persistence or revival of Pauline truth. It was almost eclipsed before Paul himself was taken from the scene. We seldom read of it in ecclesiastical histories, as it made little impression on the times. There were feeble flickers among the Waldensians in Switzerland, and the Hussites in Bohemia; Luther and his helpers recovered a little in Germany; Wycliffe and Darby in England made some advance; but in almost *every* case there was no clearcut severance from the Circumcision Scriptures, and these dominated and darkened the light. ...

... [T]he great mass of those who are saved in this administration neither know nor appreciate the favor which fashions their fate. Nay, most of them actively disown it and denounce those who seek to reveal it to them. They are saved by a grace which they detest, for it takes away from them the robe of their own righteousness.[9]

---

9. A.E. Knoch, *The Problem of Evil,* pp. 270ff, Concordant Publishing Concern, 2008.

II Timothy Chapter 1

PAUL'S UNIQUE APOSTLESHIP

Paul, an apostle of Jesus Christ by the will of God, according to the promise of life which is in Christ Jesus (II Timothy 1:1).

Paul was *not* one of the Twelve Apostles: he had a unique, special Apostleship from the Lord Jesus Christ.

Paul Was Not Chosen During Christ's Earthly Ministry

The twelve Apostles were chosen in Matthew chapter ten.

Now the names of the twelve apostles are these; the first, Simon, who is called Peter, and Andrew his brother; James the son of Zebedee, and John his brother; Philip, and Bartholomew; Thomas, and Matthew the publican; James the son of Alphaeus, and Lebbaeus, whose surname was Thaddaeus; Simon the Canaanite, and Judas Iscariot, who also betrayed Him. These twelve Jesus sent forth ... (Matthew 10:2-5).

Paul Was Not Chosen as Judas's Replacement

God chose Matthias as the replacement for Judas.

And they prayed, and said, "You, Lord, Who knows the hearts of all men, show whether of these two You have chosen, that he may take part of this ministry and apostleship, from which Judas by transgression fell, that he might go to his own place." And they gave forth their lots; and the lot fell upon Matthias; and he was numbered with the eleven apostles (Acts 1:24-26).

Paul Did Not Meet the Requirements to Be One of the Twelve

There were very specific and detailed requirements for being one of the twelve. Paul did not meet these requirements.

Wherefore of these men which have companied with us all the time that the Lord Jesus went in and out among us, beginning from the baptism of John, unto that same day that he was taken up from us, must one be ordained to be a witness with us of His resurrection (Acts 1:21-22).

He would have had to have been in the *company* of the twelve *all* the time that the Lord was among them, from the *"beginning … until* the *same day"* of Christ's ascension.

Paul Received and Preached a Different Gospel than that of the Twelve Apostles

… The gospel of the Uncircumcision was committed unto me, as the gospel of the Circumcision was unto Peter (Galatians 2:7).

Paul Did Not Receive His Gospel Revelation from the Twelve Apostles

But I certify you, brothers, that the gospel which was preached of me is not after man. For I neither received it of man, neither was I taught it, but by the revelation of Jesus Christ (Galatians 1:11, 12).

Paul calls this gospel that he received by the revelation of Jesus Christ, *"my gospel."*

*In the day when God shall judge the secrets of men by Jesus Christ according to **my gospel*** (Romans 2:16).

*Now to Him Who is of power to establish you according to **my gospel,** and the preaching of Jesus Christ, according to the revelation of the mystery, which was kept secret in ages past ...* (Romans 16:25-26).

Paul Had an Apostleship Distinct from the Twelve Apostles

Peter and the Twelve were Apostles to the Circumcision – the Jews – while Paul was the Apostle to the Gentiles – the Nations (Paul was God's *international* apostle).

... He Who wrought effectually in Peter to the Apostleship of the Circumcision, the same was mighty in me toward the Gentiles ... (Galatians 2:8).

For I speak to you Gentiles, inasmuch as I am the Apostle of the Gentiles, I magnify my office (Romans 11:13).

PAUL'S GRACE APOSTLESHIP

Paul, an apostle of Jesus Christ by the will of God, according to the promise of life which is in Christ Jesus (II Timothy 1:1).

Not only was Paul *not* one of *"the Twelve"* Apostles, he also was given a new message, about a new dispensation, with a new commission, resulting in the forming and building of a new people.

Paul Ministered a New Message

Paul did not preach what *"the Twelve"* taught. Rather, he preached the gospel of the grace of God.

There are many gospels in the Bible. Paul was chosen to testify of *"the gospel of the grace of God."*

> *... The ministry, which I have received of the Lord Jesus, to testify the gospel of the grace of God* (Acts 20:24).

This gospel did not come to Paul from others; it was a divine revelation.

> *... I certify you, brothers, that the gospel which was preached of me is not after man. For I neither received it of man, neither was I taught it, but by the revelation of Jesus Christ* (Galatians 1:11-12).

So much was this a new message that Paul had to make a trip to Jerusalem to tell them of this heavenly revelation.

> *... I went up by revelation, and communicated unto them that gospel which I preach among the Gentiles ... for they who seemed to be somewhat in conference added nothing to me: but contrariwise, when they saw that the Gospel of*

the Uncircumcision was committed unto me, as the Gospel of the Circumcision was unto Peter (Galatians 2:2-7).

Notice that Paul called this new gospel *"the Gospel of the Uncircumcision."* He also called it distinctly his gospel – *i.e., "my gospel."*

In the day when God shall judge the secrets of men by Jesus Christ according to my gospel (Romans 2:16).

Now to Him Who is of power to establish you according to my gospel (Romans 16:25).

Remember that Jesus Christ of the seed of David was raised from the dead according to my gospel (II Timothy 2:8).

This was a new message *"which was kept secret in ages past."*

Now to Him Who is of power to establish you according to my gospel, and the preaching of Jesus Christ, according to the revelation of the mystery, which was kept secret in ages past (Romans 16:25).

Paul Ministered in a New Dispensation

Paul's good news was a part of a revelation of a whole new divine administration with mankind – the unreserved dispensing of God's grace.

If you have heard of the dispensation of the grace of God which is given me to you (Ephesians 3:2).

Whereof I am made a minister, according to the dispensation of God which is given to me for you, to fulfill the Word of God; even the mystery which has been hidden from ages and from generations, but now is made manifest to His saints: to whom God would make known what is the riches of the glory of this mystery among the Gentiles; which is Christ in you, the hope of glory (Colossians 1:25-27).

Paul Ministered with a New Commission

Paul did not labor under Israel's so-called "Great Commission." The commission of Paul's Gospel was grandly different.

For Christ sent me not to baptize, but to preach the gospel … (I Corinthians 1:17).

And all things are of God, Who has reconciled us to Himself by Jesus Christ, and has given to us the ministry of reconciliation; to wit, that God was in Christ, reconciling the world unto Himself, not imputing their trespasses unto them; and has committed unto us the Word of reconciliation. Now then we are ambassadors for Christ, as though God did beseech you by us: we pray you in Christ's stead, be reconciled to God. For He has made Him to be sin for us, Who knew no sin; that we might be made the righteousness of God in Him (II Corinthians 5:18-21).

Paul Ministered to a New People

Unlike *"the Twelve"* who ministered to Israel, Paul ministered to the newly formed Body of Christ, the heavenly creation. All earthly, fleshly distinction was now gone.

Wherefore henceforth know we no man after the flesh: yea, though we have known Christ after the flesh, yet now henceforth know we Him no more. Therefore if any man is in Christ, he is a new creature: old things are passed away; behold, all things are become new (II Corinthians 5:16-17).

For by one Spirit are we all baptized into one Body, whether we are Jews or Gentiles, whether we are bond or free ... Now you are the Body of Christ, and members in particular (I Corinthians 12:13, 27).

PROMISE OF LIFE IN CHRIST JESUS

Paul, an apostle of Jesus Christ by the will of God, according to the promise of life which is in Christ Jesus (II Timothy 1:1).

How amazing it is that a man sentenced to die would start out talking about LIFE! Still, Paul knew his source of life: *"the promise of life which is in Christ Jesus."* The person of the Lord Jesus Christ was his hope! He was the promise of life! Christ was Paul's Life and is ours as well. *"Christ, Who is our life ..."* (Colossians 3:4).

This promise of life finds its fulfillment in *resurrection.* There lies the believer's hope against *"the sentence of death"* which resides upon all of us.

But we had the sentence of death in ourselves, that we should not trust in ourselves, but in God Who raises the dead (II Corinthians 1:9).

Our trust is not *"in ourselves"*: it is *"in God Who raises the dead."* The demonstration and assurance of that hope is in the resurrection of our Lord and Savior, Jesus Christ.

... He has given assurance unto all men, in that He has raised Him from the dead (Acts 17:31).

Herein lies *"the promise of life"* ... even to an old man facing execution – it is *"Christ Jesus!"*

DON'T BE AFRAID, DON'T BE ASHAMED

For God has not given us the spirit of fear; but of power, and of love, and of a sound mind. Be not therefore ashamed of the testimony of our Lord, nor of me His prisoner: but be partaker of the afflictions of the gospel according to the power of God (II Timothy 1:7-8).

Two of the greatest tools of the enemy, used against Timothy, were *"fear"* (1:7) and *"shame"* (1:8). This was brought to the forefront in Timothy's life because of the situation in which Paul found himself – in prison.

Andre Sneidar has written,

It seems that Timothy may have been intimidated by those who had prestige, power and influence within the arena of religion and politics, and possibly brought pressure to bear against him.

Stuart Allen has written,

The Apostle was now living for the most part in loneliness and rejection. Imprisonment for the truth evidently carried with it a social stigma, and the danger of giving public witness to the religion that was now illicit made the possibility of shame a real one.[10]

The Adversary still uses these tactics – fear and shame – as his greatest resources. How many believers have been silenced and their lives made ineffectual by these oppressions? These are mental war games from the hand of the adversary (*c.f.* II Corinthians 10:4-5), but Paul reminds Timothy that he has been given the divine spirit of power and love, and a sound mind:

I thank God ... that without ceasing I have remembrance

---

10. Stuart Allen, *Letters From Prison.*

*of you in my prayers night and day; Greatly desiring to see you, being mindful of **your tears,** that I may be filled with joy* (II Timothy 1:3-4).

*For God has not given us the spirit of **fear** ... **Be not therefore ashamed** of the testimony of our Lord, nor of me His prisoner ...* (II Timothy 1:7-8).

That the fear of such intimidation was widespread is evidenced by the following passages:

*This you know, that **all they who are in Asia are turned away from me** ...* (II Timothy 1:15).

*For **Demas has forsaken me,** having loved this present world, and is departed unto Thessalonica; Crescens to Galatia, Titus unto Dalmatia* (II Timothy 4:10).

*At my first answer **no man stood with me, but all men forsook me:** I pray God that it may not be laid to their charge* (II Timothy 4:16).

Paul's instruction to Timothy was tender:

For God has not given us the spirit of fear; but of power, and of love, and of a sound mind (II Timothy 1:7)."

Timothy may have been on the verge of a "nervous breakdown," of "losing his mind," so intense was the pressure upon him; but he did not need a psychologist or psychiatrist to get through this sorrow, timidity, depression and despair. God had already given him all the provision he needed – *"a sound mind"* (1:7).

NOT ASHAMED

*Be not therefore ashamed of the testimony of our Lord,
nor of me His prisoner: but be partaker of the afflictions of
the gospel according to the power of God* (II Timothy 1:8).

This idea of shame was such a big one that it is a reccuring
theme in this first chapter.

– Timothy was not to be ashamed (1:8).
– Paul was not ashamed (1:12).
– The house of Onesiphorus was not ashamed (1:16).

Timothy was exhorted not to be ashamed. He was not to be
ashamed of our Lord, nor His testimony; neither was he to be
ashamed of Paul. To be ashamed of Paul is to be ashamed of
the Lord! Paul is God's divinely appointed representative and
spokesman for the Body of Christ in *"the dispensation of the
grace of God,"* just as Moses had been for Israel under the
law. Paul is the Apostle to the Nations (Romans 11:13), and
encourages Timothy not to be ashamed of him, even though
he was in prison as an evil-doer (1:8; 2:9). After all, Paul was
not ashamed of the degrading circumstances in which he found
himself imprisoned.

*For the which cause I also suffer these things: nevertheless
I am not ashamed: for I know Whom I have believed, and
am persuaded that He is able to keep that which I have
committed unto Him against that day* (II Timothy 1:12).

In spite of all of the things that had, and were transpiring, Paul
had a firm confidence. In the midst of what could have been
great humiliation, disgrace, embarrassment and shame, Paul
knew Whom he believed. Paul's confidence was not just in *what*
he believed, but in *Whom!* It was not about Paul at all – rather,
it was about His able, faithful Lord. Paul sought to encourage
Timothy by his own example. Paul's confidence was in the
person of the Lord Jesus Christ!

However, Paul did not stop there, as he also shared Onesiphorus as an example.

> *The Lord give mercy unto the house of Onesiphorus; for he oft refreshed me, and was not ashamed of my chain* (II Timothy 1:16).

We know so very little about Onesiphorus, but it is obvious that Timothy knew him well, as Paul displayed him as an example of faith and spiritual courage. As E.W. Bullinger has written, Onesiphrous "must have recently died,"[11] and Paul speaks of his faithfulness to the very end.

It is amazing that, in the middle of the greatest crisis of Paul's own life, we see his great love and compassion, not only for Timothy, but also for the family of Onesiphorus – *"the Lord give mercy upon the house of Onesiphorus."*

---

11. E.W. Bullinger, *The Companion Bible*, p. 1810.

PARTAKERS OF THE AFFLICTIONS OF THE GOSPEL

*Be not therefore ashamed of the testimony of our Lord,
nor of me His prisoner: but be partaker of the afflictions of
the gospel according to the power of God* (II Timothy 1:8).

Paul encourages Timothy to be a co-sufferer with him; to join
with him in the patient suffering and endurance of evil for the
sake of God's glorious and gracious good news.

A.E. Knoch wrote wonderfully of this calling of all those who
will be true to the message delivered to Paul:

> Those who spread Paul's teaching must suffer Paul's treatment.
> The teaching and the treatment are close companions. The
> more gain you deserve at the dais [Judgment Seat of Christ]
> the more pain you are likely to bear beforehand. Paul's
> case was not due to his person, but his message. The more
> you think about it, the stranger it seems that he exhorts his
> successor to *suffer evil!* How seldom is this note heard today
> in preparing for the ministry! Is it not because Paul's message
> is missing? … [W]hen we are faithful to Paul's evangel, and
> the inevitable evil ensues, let us bear it and never shrink
> from suffering *with* the great herald and apostle and teacher.
> Rather, let us cherish it as a privilege, the highest honor which
> this era can confer on the sons of Adam.[12]

---

12. A.E. Knoch, *The Problem of Evil,* pp 270ff, Concordant Publishing Concern,
    2008.

HOLD ON TO PAUL'S WORDS

Paul encourages Timothy to *"hold fast the form of sound words, which you have heard of me"* (1:13). Paul presents his epistles as the divine pattern. Timothy was exhorted not to abandon the actual words of Paul for some new, improved, "politically correct," "ecclesiastically correct" ones. The actual recorded words of Paul are the divine standard of our dispensation. "Standard" is found in the definition of this word *"form."*[13] In the *King James Version* it is translated *"pattern"* in I Timothy 1:16.

> *Howbeit for this cause I obtained mercy, that in me first Jesus Christ might show forth all longsuffering, for **a pattern** to them who should hereafter believe on Him to age-lasting life* (I Timothy 1:16).

Paul's epistles are the divine standard of truth for our age. Everything must be measured accordingly, whether by teaching or practice!

D.L. McCroskey wrote,

> Timothy is urged to hold fast the great truths of the One Body which Paul has taught him. ... Again, it was the special revelation of the *"mystery,"* the sacred secret for this age, which Paul had committed to Timothy.[14]

Thus when Paul speaks of his words being the *"pattern"* to follow, he is referring to the actual Greek words that God had inspired him to deliver. He obviously was not making reference to the words of *other men*. When men attempt to translate the words of Paul into their language, no matter how noble their efforts, it is still the actual words of Paul that remain the divine standard.

---

13. Arndt and Gingrich's *Greek-English Lexicon.*
14. D.L. McCroskey, *II Timothy – The Divine Outline of World Apostasy* (The Last Day Messenger, November-December, 1975).

Many men blindly follow the words of their translators and, sadly, far too often they are led astray. Little wonder that we are instructed not merely to *"read,"* but to *"study."* After all, any translation of Paul's words are simply study tools at best.

These words of Paul are actually the words of our Father. Cherish them, study them, know them, proclaim and herald them, protect and defend them.

ALL HEARD; ALL TURNED AWAY

Paul spent two years teaching in the capital city of the Roman province of Asia, the result of which was that, *"all they which dwelt in Asia heard the Word of the Lord Jesus"* (Acts 19:10).

Now, sadly he states that, *"all they which are in Asia are turned away from me"* (1:15) – the church in Asia was in wholesale apostasy.

Turned Away from Paul

The Asian saints had turned away from Paul. This was an apostasy from Paul's divinely bestowed revelation and authority. This was what was at issue; it was what had been forsaken. They had not abandoned "Christendom" (in fact they were establishing it!), but they had abandoned Paul.

To abandon Paul – the messenger of the risen, ascended, glorified, enthroned Lord Jesus Christ, Who had sent him – is to abandon the Savior Himself. That makes it a serious matter.

> *Verily, verily, I say unto you, "He who receives whomsoever I send receives Me; and he who receives Me receives Him Who sent Me"* (John 13:20).

To disregard the importance of Paul's apostleship is to bring about disaster. Those in the *"Asia"* of biblical times *turned* away from Paul (II Timothy 1:15) and were themselves *turned* unto fables (*c.f.* II Timothy 4:4). Even after over nineteen centuries, the people occupying this area are still in spiritual darkness.

The answers to the current ills and "isms" of the church are to be found in Pauline truth. Paul says to us,

> *Be followers of me, even as I also am of Christ* (I Corinthians 11:1).

Christ is our goal; Paul is our guide.

> The only hope of Christianity is in the rehabilitating of Pauline theology. It is back, back, back to an incarnate Christ and the atoning blood, or it is on, on, on to atheism and despair.[15]

---

15. Francis L. Patton (1843-1932), president of Princeton University, 1888-1902.

II Timothy Chapter 2

BE STRONG IN GRACE

Therefore, my son, be strong in the grace that is in Christ Jesus (II Timothy 2:1).

Because of this condition of apostasy in the Body of Christ (*"therefore"* – 2:1), Paul admonished Timothy to *"be strong in the grace that is in Christ Jesus."* The answer to standing would be found in God's grace. Grace is where Timothy needed to find his strength, to be strong, where he needed his focus and emphasis to be. Paul could tell this to Timothy, not as just a theory, but as a way – *the* way – of life. Paul had firsthand experience with the power of grace.

For this thing I besought the Lord thrice, that it might depart from me. And He said unto me, "My grace is sufficient for you: for My strength is made perfect in weakness." Most gladly therefore will I rather glory in my infirmities, that the power of Christ may rest upon me. Therefore I take pleasure in infirmities, in reproaches, in necessities, in persecutions, in distresses for Christ's sake: for when I am weak, then am I strong (II Corinthians 12:8-10).

Be strong in grace – this is the appeal; and this is the Pauline pattern. The strong part of our lives needs to be God's grace; this is where we are to focus and excel.

Moreover the law entered, that the offense might abound. But where sin abounded, grace did much more abound: That as sin has reigned unto death, even so might grace reign through righteousness unto eternal life by Jesus Christ our Lord (Romans 5:20-21).

TEACH FAITHFUL MEN

And the things that you have heard of me among many witnesses, the same commit to faithful men, who shall be able to teach others also (II Timothy 2:2).

Paul's instruction to Timothy is of a very personal and individual nature throughout this epistle. The believers in Asia were now outside of the teachings and practices of Paul. They had turned away from him. They were now embracing the religious system; a "Christian" religious system – "Christendom." Without Paul's message, that is all one has – RELIGION.

Timothy therefore now finds himself on the *outside* of the activities of the believers. Interestingly enough, Paul never instructs Timothy anywhere in this epistle to "go in" among them and see if he could "turn the tide." Instead of ministering to "a congregation," "a church," "an assembly" or "his parishioners," Paul tells Timothy to *"find faithful men."* Timothy was to seek out men, *"faithful men"* to whom he could commit Paul's message.

Paul had no thought of Asia ever being "revived." Instead, because of the apostasy, his instruction to Timothy concerning the ministry of the Word had now become extremely narrow, intensely individual – *"faithful men!"*

The importance of faithfulness can be seen clearly in I Corinthians 4:2.

Moreover it is required in stewards, that a man be found faithful.

Paul did not want Timothy to spend his time and energy on "groups" and "congregations" of men who were not faithful to the Lord and His message. Timothy was not instructed to teach the "masses."

E.W. Bullinger comments on this passage, that there is "No reference to bishops and ecclesiastical organizations."[16]

What a shame to look around at all the so-called "churches" filled with unfaithful men, and see all the energy, money, resources and programs trying to allure them into becoming "regular" attendees. Does this not show us how far we have turned away from Paul?

What was Timothy instructed to commit to these *"faithful men?"*

Ordination?
Creeds?
Articles of Faith?
Statements of Faith?
Business Meetings?
Church Polity?
Sunday School Administration?
Preparation and Delivery of Sermons?

NO!

He was to commit to these *"faithful men"* the very things that he had heard from Paul! Once again Paul's distinct message is being brought to its paramount place. Paul says **"the same commit to faithful men"** (2:2). He does not say "similar."

Andre Sneidar has written,

> Timothy's duty now is to seek out faithful men, wherever he may be able to find them, and instruct them individually, and they in turn will go forth doing the same.

16. *The Companion Bible*, p. 1810).

EXAMPLES FOR TIMOTHY

Paul had encouraged Timothy to *"be strong in the grace that is in Christ Jesus"* (2:1). Timothy would need this, because he was going to have to *"endure hardness."* Things were not going to get any easier for him. It was going to be very hard. The same is true for us. If we are committed to a life dedicated to Paul's gospel, never imagine that life will one day get easier; far from it.

Paul uses three examples to illustrate the endurance, faithfulness and patience that were needed for the days of ruin:

Example	Difficulty	Character	Goal
Soldier	Hardness	Endurance	Please Him
Athlete	Strive	Faithfulness	Crown
Farmer	Labor	Patience	First Partaker

Concerning these three areas A.E. Knoch wrote:

This group of figures, which applies to all who belong to Christ in this administration … includes nothing but the *suffering* of a soldier, the *rules* of the games, and the *first*ness of the farmer in partaking of his fruits.[17]

---

17. A.E. Knoch, *The Problem of Evil*, p. 275, Concordant Publishing Concern, 2008.

THE SUFFERING SOLDIER

Therefore endure hardness, as a good soldier of Jesus Christ. No man who wars entangles himself with the affairs of this life; that he may please Him Who has chosen Him to be a soldier (II Timothy 2:3-4).

There is nothing easy about the life of a believer, especially one dedicated to the truth of Paul's gospel. This is why Paul exhorted Timothy to *"endure hardness."* Hardness: it had been hard; it was hard; it would be hard.

We will again enjoy the insight of A.E. Knoch:

Timothy was not exhorted to emulate a soldier in *every* particular. He was not advised to take physical training to build up his bodily strength and learn how to fight and destroy and kill his enemies – quite the opposite! Yet there was one phase of the soldier's life which would enter his experience, and that is *suffering*. We seldom picture an ideal soldier as a sufferer. We paint him as in the prime of youthful strength and vigor, with martial might, as the song says, "marching as to war." If I had any idea that it would be accepted, I would suggest that these words be changed to a more scriptural phrase, *"suffering* as *in* war," but who would want to *sing* about that? Alas, the "Christian soldiers" of today do not take their marching orders from Paul, so have little cause to suffer.

Millions upon millions of men living today have learned that Paul was right. The false glamour of war has been replaced in their minds by the realities of its results. What *suffering* has followed in its train! Hitherto there seems to have been little recognition of this aspect in military circles. Bravery and success were rewarded with medals and decorations, as they are now, but today wounds and suffering call for stripes [awards] and the purple heart. Whatever may be the outward symbols of combat, the most enduring are engraved in the hearts of those who suffered fatigue and hunger, disease and mutilation, nerve shock and utter spiritual devastation. Such is the picture put before us by Paul. Just as some of the soldiers who suffered severely cheerfully faced their fate, so we should accept the suffering which comes to us, with Paul, with acquiescent fortitude and thankfulness.[18]

---

18. A.E. Knoch, *The Problem of Evil,* pp. 274, 275, Concordant Publishing Concern, 2008.

THE FAITHFUL ATHLETE

And if a man also strives for masteries, yet is he not crowned, except he strives lawfully (II Timothy 2:5).

An athlete can't compete in a game just anyway he wants, making up the rules as he goes. He must follow the rules of the game or be disqualified. The same is true with the believer. He must know what God's program for this age is, and he must follow its "rules" to win the race and prize.

A.E. Knoch writes,

> [The athlete] races and boxes so as not to be *disqualified* (*"castaway"* – I Corinthians 9:27). He must observe the rules of the game. An athlete who fails to observe the conditions would be disqualified – he loses the race even if he is first over the line. He is not acclaimed the winner in a boxing match if he strikes below the belt. So it will be at the dais.[19]

C.R. Stam also writes,

> The racer cannot decide to start running *just before* the signal, so as to get a head start! The participants in athletic competition *must abide by the rules of the game or be immediately disqualified.* In each game the rules are different from all the rest: tennis is different from baseball, and soccer from both, but in each case the participants *must abide by the rules* for *that* game ...
>
> This is important, for there are many Christians who do indeed make their own rules where doctrine and service are concerned. Think of the great attempt to return to Pentecost and its miraculous demonstrations! Pentecost was a fulfillment *of prophecy,* and the antitype of all the Pentecosts that had

---

19. A.E. Knoch, *The Problem of Evil,* p. 275, Concordant Publishing Concern, 2008.

gone before. It was *"when THE day of Pentecost* [the great antitype] *had **fully** come"* that the gift of tongues and other miraculous signs of our Lord's Messiahship were granted …

Others make their own rules where the so-called "Great Commission" is concerned. They just decide for themselves *which record* of the commission is to be obeyed, and even *which parts* of any or all of them apply to the present dispensation. This is a simple case of making one's own rules …

The Christian has *no right* to make his own rules, and this applies especially to those who minister the Word. He must go by the written Word of God, "rightly divided," or be disqualified from the contest (See I Corinthians 9:27, and *c.f.* II Timothy 2:15, where the word "castaway" and "approved" are the very opposite in the Greek: *adokimos* and *dokimos,* referring to the disapproval or the approval of participants *in the contest* – not, thank God, as His redeemed children).

How important, then, to heed the words of Paul in I Corinthians 3:10: *"According to the grace of God which is given unto me as a wise masterbuilder, I have laid the foundation and another builds thereon. But let every man take heed how he builds thereupon."*

Do not decide for yourself that it is all right to build Mosaic or Petrine material on the Pauline foundation. Do not preach the Law, the Sermon on the Mount, or the Gospel of the Kingdom instead of the message we have been *commissioned* to proclaim: Christ, according to *"the revelation of the mystery, which was kept secret since the world began, but now is made manifest"* (Romans 16:25-26). If you fail to proclaim this gospel, unmixed with messages for other ages, depend upon it: you will *not "receive a reward"* at the Judgment Seat of Christ … (Read carefully I Corinthians 3:10-15).[20]

---

20. C.R. Stam, *The Pastoral Epistles*, p. 150, Berean Bible Society.

THE FRUITFUL FARMER

The husbandman who labors must be first-partaker of the fruits (II Timothy 2:6).

Many seem to think that they will reap spiritual things without sowing spiritual seed. It is the farmer who first enjoys the fruit of his labors. Though we may enjoy the fruit of another's labors, the fruit actually belongs to them.

We hear again from C.R. Stam:

The "husbandman," of course, is the *farmer,* and who will question that he *should* be the first to partake of the fruits of his labor? He must spend long hours toiling in the field, plowing, sowing, reaping. Thus as in the *steward* God looks for fidelity and ability, as in the *soldier* He looks for courage and self-discipline, as in the *athlete* He requires conformity to the rules, so in the farmer it is "labor," diligent toil, He expects. This is what it takes to produce fruit from the ground (Genesis 3:17-19; James 5:7).

Doubtless one major reason why so many believers see so little fruit from their testimony is that they put so little into it. Others start, but soon become discouraged and settle down again into a near-useless life. Paul implies that it is natural to become weary, discouraged or disillusioned, and finally to give up, as he exhorts, *"Therefore, my beloved brethren, be ye steadfast, unmoveable, always abounding in the work of the Lord, forasmuch as ye know that your labor is not in vain in the Lord"* (I Corinthians 15:58).

But not only is our labor *"not in vain in the Lord,"* since He honors faithfulness, unremitting toil in His service also insures eventual reaping. This is a scriptural promise that few have recognized. In his epistle to the Galatians the Apostle emphasizes the relationship between personal, individual toil and personal reaping: *"And let us not be weary in well doing, for in due season WE shall reap IF we faint not"* (Galatians 6:9).[21]

21. C.R. Stam, *The Pastoral Epistles*, p. 151, Berean Bible Society.

THE MYSTERY OF PAUL'S GOSPEL
*The Sacred Secret Revealed
Through the Evangel Committed to Paul*

*Remember that Jesus Christ, descended from David, was raised from the dead according to **my gospel** (II Timothy 2:8).*

Paul's *"my gospel"* was firmly centered in the *"preaching"* (i.e., proclaiming, heralding) of Jesus Christ. Yet Paul did not merely proclaim Jesus Christ based on His earthly ministry as recorded in the four "Gospels" of Matthew, Mark, Luke and John. Instead, he proclaimed Jesus Christ based upon an advancement in truth from God – a progression known as *"the revelation of THE MYSTERY."*

Now to Him Who is of power to establish you according to my gospel, and the preaching of Jesus Christ, according to the revelation of the mystery, which was kept secret in ages past (Romans 16:25).

Why Is It Called *"THE MYSTERY"*?

Because it was "Kept Secret."

*... The revelation of the mystery, which was **kept secret** in ages past (Romans 16:25).*

Because it was "Hidden in God."

*... The fellowship of the mystery, which from the beginning of the world has been **hidden in God** ... (Ephesians 3:9).*

Because it was "Hidden from Ages and from Generations."

*Even the mystery which has been **hidden from ages and from generations** ... (Colossians 1:26).*

*Which **in other ages was not made known** unto the sons of men ...* (Ephesians 3:5).

Because it was "Unsearchable."

*... That I should preach among the Gentiles the **unsearchable** riches of Christ* (Ephesians 3:8).

Paul's message was *"unsearchable,"* i.e., it was untraceable – not locatable – in the rest of Scripture. (For a further look at *"the mystery"* study the following references: Ephesians 1:9; 3:3-4; 6:19; Colossians 4:3; I Timothy 3:9.)

Where Did THE MYSTERY Originate?

It Came as a Direct, Divine Revelation.

I certify you, brothers, that the gospel which was preached of me is not after man. For I neither received it of man, neither was I taught it, but by the revelation of Jesus Christ (Galatians 1:11-12).

... By revelation He made known to me The Mystery ... (Ephesians 3:3).

... I will come to visions and revelations of the Lord ... the abundance of the revelations ... (II Corinthians 12:1, 7).

The last words of the Lord Jesus Christ are not recorded in the book of Acts (chapter one).

To Whom Was THE MYSTERY Revealed?

Paul was the Recipient of THE MYSTERY.

... The gospel of the uncircumcision was committed unto me ... (Galatians 2:7).

... The dispensation of the grace of God which is given me ... (Ephesians 3:2).

... The dispensation of God which is given to me ... (Colossians 1:25).

... The gospel which was preached of me is not after man ... (Galatians 1:11).

Paul wrote down the words concerning our Lord Jesus Christ (I Timothy 6:3) for the Body of Christ in this dispensation of Grace (Ephesians 3:2).

Paul was an apostle of the Lord (Galatians 1:15-16; 2:8; Acts 9:15; I Timothy 2:7; II Timothy 1:11; Acts 26:16-17; Romans 11:13; 15:16).

What Does THE MYSTERY Contain?

The Formation of the Body of Christ.

No other Bible author speaks of the Body of Christ.

Until Paul's reception of the revelation of *the mystery*, Israel had been the instrument of God. Now a new group of individuals, called out from among the nations, is being formed as the instrument of God (I Corinthians 10:17; 12:27; Ephesians 1:22-23; 4:4, 12; Romans 12:5; Colossians 1:18; 3:15).

This body of individuals is made up of Jews *and* Gentiles (Ephesians 2:14-18; 3:6), and begins with Paul (I Timothy 1:13-16). The body of Christ is God's *ecclesia* ("the church" – Ephesians 1:22-23; 5:23; Colossians 1:18, 24). The body of Christ is a totally new creation (Ephesians 2:15; Galatians 6:15; II Corinthians 5:17).

The Present Dispensation (i.e., Administration) of Grace.

No other Bible author speaks of this dispensation.

This dispensation begins with Paul (Ephesians 3:2; Colossians 1:25). Grace has such control in this dispensation that it is said to *"reign"* (Romans 5:21).

The Gospel of the Grace of God.

No other Bible author speaks of this gospel.

This wonderful gospel emphasizes and magnifies God's grace. Paul uses the word "grace" over 100 times in his epistles (more than any other Bible author.) This gospel was provided for by the finished redemptive work of the Lord Jesus Christ, but it was not revealed until Paul (I Timothy 2:5-7; II Timothy 1:9-11).

The Justification of the Believer.

The mystery reveals that the believer, joined with Christ, has been made "righteous" – and not just any righteousness, as good as that would be – we have been *"made the righteousness of God in Him* [Christ].*"* Being justified is a great advancement over just having one's sins forgiven.

The Temporary Setting Aside of Israel.

The revelation of *the mystery* gives the only scriptural answer to why God is not now dealing with the nation of Israel (Romans 11:11-15, 25). In the program of the *"kingdom of heaven"* the Gentiles were to be blessed by Israel's rise (Isaiah 11:1, 10). Yet, according to *the mystery,* the Gentiles are blessed through the *fall* of Israel.

The One Baptism.

There were *"diverse"* (many) baptisms under God's program for Israel (Hebrews 6:2; 9:10). By contrast, the revelation of *the mystery* has only *ONE* baptism, which is spiritual (Ephesians 4:4; I Corinthians 12:13; Romans 6:3; Galatians 3:27; Colossians 2:12; I Corinthians 1:17).

The Heavenly Position of the Body of Christ.

Whereas Israel's hope was an earthly one, *the mystery* reveals a heavenly hope for the believers in this age (Ephesians 1:3; 2:6; Philippians 3:20; Colossians 3:1-3).

AS AN EVIL DOER

Remember that Jesus Christ of the seed of David was raised from the dead according to my gospel: wherein I suffer trouble, as an evil doer, even unto bonds; but the Word of God is not bound (II Timothy 2:8-9).

It was Paul's distinct *"my gospel"* (:8) that got him into his Roman troubles. Note: *"my gospel:* **wherein** *I suffer trouble"*

At the time of his writing, Paul was imprisoned under the great persecution of Nero. Only "approved" religions were accepted and allowed to practice legally under Roman authority. Christianity at first was allowed under the assumed auspices of Judaism, but as the two were shown to be distinct and separate by Paul's teaching, his message and ministry became illegal. So, it was the very message of Paul that got him into his troubles. Now Paul, even with his privileged Roman citizenship, was in bonds, suffering, and awaiting death as *"an evil doer"* (:9). Therefore, suffering and endurance are seen as the characteristics of those who follow Paul's *"my gospel"* – even to this day.

STUDY TO SHOW YOURSELF

Study to show yourself approved unto God, a workman who needs not to be ashamed, rightly dividing the Word of Truth (II Timothy 2:15).

Once again we are reminded of the personal and individual nature of this epistle. *"Study to show yourself approved unto God ..."* Timothy was to study for himself! He was to teach the faithful men to study for themselves! The result would be that he would not be *"ashamed."* This is the "how" to Paul's instruction to him in chapter one (*"Be not therefore ashamed ..."* *"... I am not ashamed ..."*). The method of his Bible study would be *"rightly dividing the Word of Truth."* Once again the importance of Paul's distinct written revelation to the Body of Christ is stressed.

C.R. Stam shares these words,

> In a very real sense those who serve God should be craftsmen. And how does one become a spiritual craftsman [*i.e.,* *"workman"*] skilled in his understanding and teaching of the Word of God? This is by no means just a gift. It takes *"study."* The word in the Greek means to *"agonize,"* to apply oneself wholly to getting a thing done well, hence to diligently study the Word.[22]

---

22. C.R. Stam, *The Pastoral Epistles*, p. 151, Berean Bible Society.

A THREEFOLD DIVISION

Study to show yourself approved unto God, a workman who needs not to be ashamed, rightly dividing the Word of Truth (II Timothy 2:15).

An important aspect of *"rightly dividing the Word of Truth"* has to do with knowing where one fits into God's timetable of events. God's dealings with man have undergone various designed changes throughout history. Identifying and understanding these changes is basic to *"rightly dividing the Word of Truth."*

Timothy was at Ephesus, and Paul had written earlier to the Ephesians to give them a panoramic view of God's dealings with mankind through the ages. He did this by making a clear, distinct and easily identifiable threefold division. A divine timetable can be found in Ephesians 2:7-13.

Past: *"time past"* (:11)
Present: *"but now"* (:13)
Future: *"ages to come"* (:7)

In providing the Ephesians with this overview, Paul was demonstrating to them the importance of knowing where they were in God's plan for the ages.

Time Past

Paul tells us that during *"time past"* an unmistakable distinction was made between the *Circumcision* and the *Uncircumcision,* between Israel and the Gentiles.

Wherefore remember that you, being in time past Gentiles in the flesh, who are called Uncircumcision by that which is called the Circumcision in the flesh made by hands; that at that time you were without Christ, being aliens from the commonwealth of Israel, and strangers from the covenants of promise, having no hope, and without God in the world (:11-12).

Paul gives us certain identifiers for the period he refers to as *"time past."*

(1) Circumcision and *Uncircumcision* identified a basic physical, racial and social distinction made by God – one that was *"in the flesh"* and *"made with hands."*

(2) Gentiles were spiritually alienated from God and thus said to be *"without Christ."*

(3) This was their condition because they were *"aliens from the commonwealth of Israel and strangers from the covenants of promise."*

Whenever you find these distinctions governing the way God was working with men, you know immediately you are in *"time past."* The books of Genesis through the Book of Acts are taken up with God's *"time past"* dealings with man.

But Now

The *"but now"* period changed all that had been true in *"time past."* No longer are Gentiles considered *"far off."* This distinction has been eliminated and now *"those who were far off are made nigh."*

> *But now in Christ Jesus you who sometimes were far off are made nigh by the blood of Christ. For He is our peace, Who has made both one, and has broken down the middle wall of partition between us* (:13-14).

During the *"but now"* period there has been a change in the way God deals with the nations, because *"the middle wall of partition"* that stood between them and Israel has been *"broken* down." In the "but now" time they are dealt with on an *equal basis* and in the same manner: "*there is no difference.*"

Paul was the instrument our ascended Lord used to initiate the program of *grace* for the Gentiles by way of a message called "*the mystery*" – a secret purpose which God kept "*hidden*" in Himself until He revealed it to, and then through Paul the apostle.

Our Lord set the nation of Israel aside during the period covered by the book of Acts and from heaven's glory introduced a *new* program through a *new* apostle. With the revelation of this new program we move into the "*but now*" period. *Romans through Philemon* are the books that *fit* into the "*but now*" division. These are the books that detail what God is doing during the present age of the dispensation of grace.

The Ages to Come

After the present age of the dispensation of grace is brought to a close, there is still much that God will accomplish. Since His *prophetic* program for the nation Israel has currently been interrupted so that He could form the Body of Christ, His next order of business will be its completion.

Appropriately, the grouping of books following the Pauline epistles are the *Circumcision Epistles* (Hebrews through Revelation). They fit doctrinally into the "*ages to come.*" The distinction between the *Circumcision* and the *Uncircumcision* returns in the Circumcision Epistles, and we find such statements as:

> *James, a servant of God and of the Lord Jesus Christ, to the **Twelve Tribes** which are scattered abroad, greeting (James 1:1).*

> *But you are a chosen generation, a **royal priesthood,** a*

holy nation, *a peculiar people* (I Peter 2:9; *c.f.* Exodus 19:5-6).

RIGHT DIVISION: THE ANSWER TO UNDERSTANDING SCRIPTURE

The Word of God itself provides us with the key to its own proper understanding through *"rightly dividing the Word of Truth."* God's ecclesia, the Body of Christ, is not the only people in the programs and purposes of God. People in other ages need Scripture to instruct them in the specifics of God's dealings with them just as we do. Remember that all the Scripture is *for* us – but it is not all *to* us, nor is it all *about* us. If we fail to recognize this important fact, we will never be able to properly understand just what God is doing today, nor will we know just what He would have us do.

DISORIENTED AND SUBVERTED

But shun profane and vain babblings: for they will increase unto more ungodliness. And their word will eat as does gangrene: of whom is Hymenaeus and Philetus; who concerning the truth have erred, saying that the resurrection is past already; and overthrow the faith of some (II Timothy 2:16-18).

In rejecting Paul and his unique message and apostleship, those in Ephesus and the rest of Asia had lost sight of who they were as the called-out ones from among "the nations." They also lost sight of God's grand purpose for the ages and where they actually fit into them.

Paul the apostle says unequivocally, *"I am the apostle of the Gentiles [i.e., the nations]."* Who, then, was their apostle? There can be no answer but that Paul was their apostle – as he is ours – for he was raised up by our ascended Lord specifically that he *"should be the minister of Jesus Christ to the Gentiles"* (Romans 15:16), calling out a people for His celestial purpose.

Abandoning Paul and his unique gospel, now the Ephesians had completely lost their way. They were so disoriented that they no longer even had the timing of the resurrection correct – essentially negating it. To teach that the resurrection had already occurred stood in contrast to the important truth of the verse before, that of *"rightly dividing the Word of Truth."* Having forsaken Paul and the truth, the resurrection was now being taught out of its proper context. By removing the resurrection from its place in the future and placing it in the past, they removed it from the realm of expectation and faith, and as a result they *"overthrew [or subverted] the faith of some."*

Sadly, for many, their faith had been subverted from the confident expectation of resurrection. The resurrection was a vital truth of anticipation taught by Paul, without which resulted in vanity (I Corinthians 15) and now "*vain babblings.*" The resurrection had become meaningless (vain) to them. They did not look to resurrection: instead the extent of their faith was now that they would go to heaven when they die, or perhaps that Christ would return and save the elect and throw the non-elect in hell.

Abraham had faith that in a future day he would have a son and that all the families of the earth would be blessed in his seed. Our faith is not only in the completed death and resurrection of Christ, but also in our redemption when He returns, ruling and reigning with Him in the ages [eons] to come. The end result of this reign will be the deliverance, reconciliation and glorious subjection of all creation back to God.

The misplacement of the resurrection stands in contrast to the glorious "*salvation which is in Christ Jesus with age-lasting* [eonian] *glory*" (:10), as well as the faithful sayings that we will be living together with Him, and reigning together with Him if we endure the suffering with Him (:11-13).

THE SURE FOUNDATION

Nevertheless the foundation of God stands sure, having this seal, "The Lord knows them who are His ..." (2:19).

Things were so bad in the religious system that had been developed in the wake of the abandonment of Paul's message that all that was left of the *"house of God"* (from I Timothy 3:15) was the foundation. All else had been destroyed. The *"evil day"* for which Paul had warned them to prepare had come (Ephesians 6:13).

This is, nonetheless, wonderful news; for, in spite of the wholesale apostasy in Asia, Paul encourages Timothy that God's firm foundation stands solid.

Paul had told the Corinthian saints,

> *For other foundation can no man lay than that is laid, which is Jesus Christ* (I Corinthians 3:11).

So, the foundation that remained in Asia was Christ! He was all that was left! Yet that was encouragement because, ultimately, He was all that Timothy needed.

> *And you are complete in Him ...* (Colossians 2:10).

Paul himself is the one who laid the foundation of Christ.

> *According to the grace of God which is given unto me, as a wise masterbuilder, I have laid the foundation* [Paul gives the Corinthians a warning with this truth] *and another builds thereon. But let every man take heed how he builds thereupon"* (I Corinthians 3:10).

Paul had laid the foundation in Asia, which was Christ, and He remained – but that is all that remained. *"The day"* had arrived in Asia, and *"every man's work"* was *"made manifest: for the day shall declare it, because it shall be revealed by fire; and the fire shall try every man's work of what sort it is"* (I Corinthians 3:13). The building in Asia had been destroyed; but Christ the foundation remained, and He still remains SURE and UNMOVABLE!

Things were so bad in the abandonment of Paul's message, that it was also hard to tell who was a saint and who was not. They had joined themselves to Rome's respected religious system. They were now a part of a mixed multitude. Paul then reminds Timothy that the Lord knows all about it, and that He knows who belongs to Him.

> *Nevertheless the foundation of God stands sure,* ***having this seal, "The Lord knows them who are His* ...***"*** (2:19).

In days of apostasy only the Lord can sort out the mess. The system isn't His, but praise the Lord, we find rest in this wonderful truth, *"the Lord knows them who are His."*

DEPART FROM RELIGIOUS INIQUITY

... And, let everyone who names the name of Christ depart from iniquity (2:19).

Now a sobering instruction comes from Paul. What is the *"iniquity"* that Paul is talking about? Is it just iniquity in general? Or, does the context lead us to a certain type of iniquity?

We will see that the next verse will provide for us the context from which to answer this important question. Paul's answer is that we who name the name of Christ should depart from RELIGIOUS iniquity!

Paul must have had in mind the parallel passage of Numbers 16:5, 26, when he wrote of the believer's departing from iniquity! Take a moment to read it.

> *And he* [Moses] *spoke unto Korah and unto all his company, saying, "Even tomorrow the LORD will show who are His, and who is holy; and will cause him to come near unto Him: even him whom He has chosen will He cause to come near unto Him ..." And he* [Moses] *spoke unto the congregation, saying, "Depart, I pray you, from the tents of these wicked men, and touch nothing of theirs, lest you be consumed in all their sins."*

Korah opposed the authority of Moses, and with his persuasive *"gainsayings"* (Jude 1:11) established a competing "tabernacle" in the wilderness.

Moses, as you know, was God's divinely appointed messenger to Israel. Korah established an imitation of the real thing, even to the point of delusion. So it is with Christendom: it withstands Paul, God's divinely appointed messenger for the Body of Christ. It too is an imitation of the real thing. The real thing is the *ecclesia*, the Body of Christ; yet Christendom presents its own versions of "church" to the point of delusion.

While it is "social" and "moral" "iniquity" with which religion is so obsessed and will try to avoid, the believer has been called to depart from the *religious iniquity*. Jesus was *"a friend of publicans and sinners,"* and it was religious leaders whom He called a *"generation of vipers."*

THE HOUSE OF GOD AND THE GREAT HOUSE

But in a great house there are not only vessels of gold and of silver, but also of wood and of earth; and some to honor, and some to dishonor (II Timothy 2:20).

Now we get to the heart of the situation in Asia. In the first epistle to Timothy, Paul talks about *"the house of God,"* identifying it as *"the church [ecclesia] of the living God, the pillar and the ground of the truth"* (I Timothy 3:15). That is simple enough! The *"house of God"* is *"the church of the living God,"* *"which is His Body"* (Ephesians 1:22-23). The *"house of God"* is the saints! It is *not* a building, *not* an organization, and it is NOT the so-called "local church."[23]

When we get to this second epistle to Timothy, Paul now talks about a contrasting *"great house"* (II Timothy 2:20). When *"the house of God"* turned from Paul, it turned to *"a great house!"* This "great house" was *not* *"the house of God."* It was "Christendom" – the natural enemy of the *true* church.

Note that :20 starts with *"But"* – *"But in a great house ..."* Therefore, this *"great house"* stands in contrast to *"the foundation"* of :19 – which is Christ. This *"great house"* has nothing to do with Him, but stands in contrast and contradiction to Him. It is built upon another foundation *other* than Christ.

The word *"great"* here in :20 is not the word for "wonderful," as when we might say, "that was a great dinner!" Instead it is the word meaning "big" (*Strong's Greek Lexicon* #3173), and is also translated *"large."* We are not dealing with what *sort* (*i.e.,* kind) of structure it was, but with its *size.* *"Sort"* (I Corinthians 3:13) is what is at issue in the building of God's house, the temple; but here is *man's* house, his substitute for the real church, where the emphasis is not on God's issue of *"sort,"* but on man's issue of

---

23. This so-called "local church" is not to be confused with *the ecclesia* in a locality!

size. When it comes to religion, *size matters.*

So we might call this *"great house"* the *"big house."* Interestingly enough, *"big house"* is what we call a PRISON! That is exactly what this house is: a prison of religious bondage!

THE GREATEST SHOW ON EARTH

But in a great house there are not only vessels of gold and of silver, but also of wood and of earth; and some to honor, and some to dishonor (II Timothy 2:20).

This *"Great House"* of religion is very impressive! After all, this is the nature of religion – it has a "grand" façade – but all that glitters is not gold, and Paul had warned of the "showy" aspect of religion when he wrote to the Galatians. He said that they

> ... *desire to make a fair **show** in the flesh* ... (Galatians 6:12).

"The Greatest Show on Earth" is the slogan of the *Ringling Brothers and Barnum & Bailey Circus;* but if the truth be known, the greatest show on earth would be Christendom's religious institutions called "church." This *"Great House"* IS earth's greatest *show*-business, and it has been giving saints the "business" for two millennia.

Do you think that this is all a little far-fetched? It isn't: there is actually an etymological connection between the Sunday morning "church" and the "circus."

One of the most popular Bible dictionaries – a standard for over one hundred years – reveals an interesting connection between the two. *Smith's Bible Dictionary,* originally published in 1884, has a very remarkable observation for us regarding the roots of our English word "church":

> The derivation of the word is generally said to be from the Greek *kuriakon,* "belonging to the Lord." But the derivation has been too hastily assumed. It is probably connected with *kirk,* the Latin *circus* – because the congregations were gathered in circles.

Interestingly, think of the parallels between the religious system's "church" and *Ringling Brothers and Barnum & Bailey's* "circus."

They both are a form of entertainment.
They both have a stage.
They both have skilled performers.
They both have a ring master.
They both have a paying audience.

(Oh, yeah – and there is a lot of "*dung*" around the place).

With all the staging, show and drama, ultimately they are both a "three-ring circus." Between the "circus" and the "church," obviously, the "church" is, in reality, the greatest *show* on earth.

*Which things have indeed a **show** of wisdom in will worship, and humility, and neglecting of the body; not in any honor to the satisfying of the flesh (Colossians 2:23).*

THE MYSTERY OF INIQUITY VS.
THE MYSTERY OF GODLINESS

But in a great house there are not only vessels of gold and of silver, but also of wood and of earth; and some to honor, and some to dishonor (II Timothy 2:20).

This *"great house"* (:20) with its *"iniquity"* (:19) is a part of the *"mystery of iniquity"* (II Thessalonians 2:7) that Satan has used to stand in contrast with, and opposition to, the one true church (*ecclesia*), which is *"the mystery of godliness"* (I Timothy 3:16).

The Mixed Multitude

This *"great house"* has a mixture of vessels in it: some to *"honor,"* and some to *"dishonor,"* like the *"mixed multitude"* of Israel. This is the old Babylonian religious system. It is the habitation of devils, every foul spirit, and every unclean and hateful bird!

> *... Babylon ... the habitation of devils, and the hold of every foul spirit, and a cage of every unclean and hateful bird. For all nations have drunk of the wine of the wrath of her fornication, and the kings of the earth have committed fornication with her, and the merchants of the earth are waxed rich through the abundance of her delicacies. And I heard another voice from heaven, saying, "Come out of her, My people, that you be not partakers of her sins, and that you receive not of her plagues. For her sins have reached unto heaven, and God has remembered her iniquities ... How much she has glorified herself, and lived deliciously ..."* (Revelation 18:2-5, 7).

Note a few things from this passage in Revelation.

First, this Babylonian system is referred to as *"her"* and *"she."* Interestingly enough, the "church" of this religious system (Christendom) is also referred to as *"her"* and *"she."* In stark contrast,

God's *ecclesia* is the *"one new man"* (Ephesians 2:15). Listen as members of Christendom say, *"the church, she is ..."*

Second, there is a clear relationship between the Babylonian religious system and the nations of the world. They are in bed together ("fornication") for mutual financial advantage, along with the merchants of the world! It is a religious-political-social-economic system.

Are you a part of a religious entity that has a relationship (fornication) with human government? A "501 c3" "Church, Inc." with "non-profit" "tax-deductable" (subsidized) exemptions?

Third, we note that there is the divine call to, *"Come out of her, My people."*

Why are God's people in her? Advantage, prestige, honor, recognition, reputation and respectability.

Yet God calls OUT His people!

Listen to Paul, our apostle, give the same warning to the Corinthians:

> *Be not unequally yoked together with unbelievers: for what fellowship has righteousness with unrighteousness? and what communion has light with darkness? And what concord has Christ with Belial? Or what part has he who believes with an infidel? And what agreement has the temple of God with idols? for you are the temple of the living God; as God has said, "I will dwell in them, and I will be their God, and they shall be My people. Wherefore come out from among them, and be separate," says the Lord, "and touch not the unclean thing; and I will receive you, And will be a Father unto you, and you shall be My sons and daughters," says the Lord Almighty. Having therefore these promises, dearly beloved, let us cleanse ourselves from all*

filthiness of the flesh and of the spirit, perfecting holiness in the fear of God (II Corinthians 6:14-7:1).

"Out" of what is Paul calling believers?

What is the *"unclean thing"* that believers are not to *"touch?"*

What is the *"filthiness of the flesh and of the spirit"* from which believers are to *"cleanse"* themselves?

It is the Gentile Babylonian religious system!

Is "your church" or "your ministry" a part of this system? Why not leave it and come out?

SELF PURGING FROM THE GREAT HOUSE

If a man therefore purge himself from these, he shall be a vessel unto honor, sanctified, and meet for the Master's use, and prepared unto every good work (II Timothy 2:21).

Now, what was Timothy's attitude to be toward this *"great house?"* Was he to go in (infiltrate) and try to turn things around? After all, there were some vessels "to honor" inside. Was he to try to "revive" it? Was he to try to get it on the right track? Was he to go in and try to minister to individuals?

No!

What was Paul's instruction?

*If a man therefore **purge himself from these,** he shall be a vessel unto honor, sanctified, and meet for the Master's use, and prepared unto every good work (II Timothy 2:21).*

We who name the name of Christ are to depart from *religious iniquity.* We are not only to purge ourselves from the vessels of *"dishonor,"* but to purge ourselves from all religious participation in the *"great house."*

Purge Out, and Purge Yourself

The word translated *"purge"*[24] is found only here and in I Corinthians 5:7. What an interesting contrast these two verses provide us! In I Corinthians, Paul instructs the saints to *"Purge out therefore …"* – a purging of one from among them – while Timothy is told to purge *himself* from the *"great house."*

Andre Sneidar writes,

It strikes me that much of preaching and teaching in the

---

24. *Strong's Greek Lexicon #1571.*

realm of the religious establishment focuses on activity that is meant to change the society in which we live, *i.e.,* that we as Christian individuals would have a "positive impact" in the social, political and financial systems which govern our society.

The fault of this kind of mentality assumes that we are part of those "systems" which govern the society in which we find ourselves. This, however, is contrary to the teaching of our apostle, Paul. As we have learned, Paul's final words, as recorded to an *individual* (and thus, *not* to "the church" at large) were, *"Flee ..."* (II Timothy 2:20). The implication is that for those faithful (*"them who are His"* – :19) who desire to be effectively used of God for His plan and purpose (*"vessel unto honor ... meet for the Master's use"* – :21), they must be separated and freed (*"purge himself"* – :21) from the base and lowly elements (*"vessels ... of wood and of earth"* – :20) which not only detract from, but indeed hinder the Master's work (*"righteousness, faith, charity, peace"* – :22), and in fact stand opposed to Him (*"oppose themselves"*[25] – :25).

---

25. *Strong's Greek Lexicon #G475: antidiatithemai* – From G473 and G1303; to *set oneself opposite,* that is, *be disputatious.*
Thayer: to place one's self in opposition, to oppose, to dispose in turn, to take in hand in turn, to retaliate.

GATHERING DURING THE APOSTASY

Flee also youthful lusts: but follow righteousness, faith, charity, peace, with them who call on the Lord out of a pure heart (II Timothy 2:22).

Charles Welch shares with us some wonderful insight,

One of the most important facts to remember in connection with any attempt to form a meeting today is the condition that corporate Christianity had reached in the days of Paul. The second epistle to Timothy reveals a church in ruins, the foundation alone remaining and exposed to view. Consequently the discipline that was possible while the church was standing can no longer be put into operation. Instead of Timothy being instructed to exercise his disciplinary powers upon others, he is urged to exercise them upon himself. The foundation itself bears the seal:

Let everyone who names the name of Christ depart from iniquity (II Timothy 2:19).

The personal note is sounded in such statements as:

If a man therefore purge himself from these [not purge others] (II Timothy 3:5).

Timothy is told to *"shun"* profane and vain babblings, to *"flee"* youthful lusts, to *"follow"* righteousness, faith, love, peace with them that call on the name of the Lord out of a pure heart. Foolish and unlearned questions he is to avoid, knowing that they *"gender strifes"* (II Timothy 2). These passages seem to indicate in a general way the mind of the Lord as to the meeting together of His people."[26]

---

26. Charles Welch, *The Berean Expositor,* Vol. XII, No. 3, March 1922.

THE OUTSIDERS

All of this boils down to the fact that *we ARE* the church. We, as the saints of God, are His *ecclesia* – we are God's *called-out* people. We're the *outsiders!* This is who and what God has made us in Christ! We're **HIS** *outsiders!*

The Hebrews were told:

> *Wherefore Jesus also … suffered without the gate. Let us go forth therefore unto Him without the camp, bearing His reproach* (Hebrews 13:12-13).

In the dispensation of grace, Jesus Christ has gone even further *"without."* Today Christ has hyper-ascended *"up far above* **all** *heavens"* (Ephesians 4:10). He now stands outside of creation! He stands there in exile, the rightful ruler of heaven and earth, and we are seated together with Him there (Ephesians 2:6), as *outsiders!* He is despised and rejected by the heavens and the earth! If we live in identification with Him, we will be despised and rejected – participating in the *"fellowship of His sufferings"* (Philippians 3:10).

If God has called us *out*, why do we want to stay *in*?

RELIGIOUS LUSTS

Flee also youthful lusts: but follow righteousness, faith, charity, peace, with them who call on the Lord out of a pure heart (II Timothy 2:22).

Paul tells Timothy to, *"Flee also youthful lusts"* (2:22), but what exactly was Paul calling Timothy to do, according to the context? From what was he to flee? Youthful lusts! What usually comes to mind when we think of this? Sexual lust often comes to mind – fornication, the raging hormones of a "teenager." Yet could this actually be lusts of another kind?

First we need to get a grip on this word *"youthful."* It must be remembered that Timothy, at the time of the writing of this epistle, had been a companion and fellow servant with Paul for about fifteen years. Now, granted, Timothy was a young man when he set out with Paul; but after fifteen years he hardly would have been a "teenager."

Is sexuality the *only* "youthful" lusts? Or, can we find these sexual lusts in the context? In fact, what is in the context that surrounds this admonition? The context is RELIGION!

Therefore, Paul was telling Timothy to flee the youthful lusts of RELIGION! How many young men, especially family men, have set their hearts to "attempt great *things* for God?" Then while ensnared in the busyness of "serving God" according to their own passionate imaginations (*i.e.,* lusts), they have neglected their primary responsibilities of being husbands and fathers. Multitudes of young men have been carried away with the biographies and examples of "great men of God," by Bible colleges, institutes, universities, and seminaries, and have been pulled into the religious system by the powerful gravity of *acceptability, honor, prestige and respectability.* Undoubtedly many of them have done so with a sincerity and love for the Lord; but the subtlety of the Adversary has used these very passions to accomplish his own purposes.

Paul verifies that these *"lusts"* are *religious* lusts, because he uses the word two more times in this epistle – and they, just like this one, are firmly planted in the context of *religion*. Let's allow Paul to define his own words:

> *Having a form of godliness, but denying the power thereof: from such turn away. For of this sort are they who creep into houses, and lead captive silly women laden with sins, led away with diverse* **lusts,** *ever learning, and never able to come to the knowledge of the truth (3:5-7).*

> *For the time will come when they will not endure sound doctrine; but after their own* **lusts** *shall they heap to themselves teachers, having itching ears; And they shall turn away their ears from the truth, and shall be turned into fables (4:3-5).*

Notice that these *lusts* have to do with RELIGIOUS instruction – with *"learning"* and *"teachers!"* (We shall talk more about this later.)

NOT ALONE

Flee also youthful lusts: but follow righteousness, faith, charity, peace, with them who call on the Lord out of a pure heart (II Timothy 2:22).

Paul did not intend for Timothy to live his life *in Christ* in seclusion. He was to *"flee also youthful lusts; **but** follow righteousness, faith, charity, peace, **WITH THEM** who call upon the Lord out of a pure heart."* Timothy was to share his life intimately with those *"who call upon the Lord out of a pure heart."* From what were their hearts to be pure? In the context, RELIGION!

Praise the Lord, when one comes out to be and to stand as who he is *in Christ* – an *outsider* – he will come to find that others are *already* there. There they are, standing and living *outside* of the religious system; and although there may not be many of them (remember that Paul's was a *"not many"* ministry anyway! – I Corinthians 1:26), they can have sweet spiritual fellowship *in Christ* – in Him alone! – even if this fellowship may have to be done by letter! That's how Paul and Timothy were enjoying Christ together!

GENTLE INSTRUCTION

But foolish and unlearned questions avoid, knowing that they do gender strifes. And the servant of the Lord must not strive; but be gentle unto all men, apt to teach, patient, in meekness instructing those who oppose themselves; if God peradventure will give them repentance to the acknowledging of the truth (II Timothy 2:23-25).

As Timothy stood outside of the religious system of his day, he would have opportunity to teach fellow-members of Christ's Body the truths of Paul's message, and, clearly, there was a proper heart-attitude (2:24-25) in which it was to be done. Even though there is conflict and persecution all around the believer in response to being outside of the system, he himself must not have a contentious spirit. He should not share his life and understanding with a spirit of strife, but in gentleness – and in patience and meekness.

Saints in Opposition

Saints who are still in the religious system, for whatever reason, are actually in opposition to truth. The religious system (the empire of man-made "churches" and "ministries") has robbed the believer of their identity *in Christ*! So, in any participation with this false system, they are actually found opposing who they are *in Christ*! They are in opposition to the truth, to those who teach the truth, and even to their true-selves. They are in opposition to the truth of God! In other words, these individuals stand in opposition to the truth of God with respect to *who they are*.

Repentance in the Body of Christ

Sadly, many dear and precious saints are in bondage to such self-opposition. We must tenderly and gently offer them *instruction* (2:25); but ultimately the only way for these prisoners of spiritual warfare to find deliverance from God is to *repent* (2:25) of their opposition to the truth. This can be done only by the *"acknowledging of the truth"* (2:25).

This passage is not a discussion of the lost, or our evangelization of them. It is a passage dealing with the on-going satanic captivity of the Body of Christ.

The *true* church needs to come to Paul's epistles and acknowledge the truth of who and what we are *in Christ*. We need to acknowledge that we are *the church – the ecclesia;* that there is only one true Body of Christ; and that the "churches" that we have built, attended and supported, and the doctrines that they teach are actually frauds. We need to acknowledge that they are satanic "snares" (2:26) that have taken us captive. We need to recognize that we have been too long in satanic captivity. We will be free *in Christ!*

II Timothy Chapter 3

IT WILL GET WORSE

This know also, that in the last days perilous times shall come (II Timothy 3:1).

Earlier Paul had reminded Timothy, *"that all they who are in Asia are turned away from me"* (1:15). He did not tell Timothy to be faithful and things would be restored. If you are looking for the *restoration* of "the early church" you will be continually frustrated and discouraged. All that faith can desire is that a remnant of *"faithful men"* will continue to come out and stand apart from the world's religious system, and in completeness and simplicity *be* who and what they are *in Christ*.

We know that this is the condition, because Paul goes on to tell us about the future of the Body of Christ. He tells Timothy that the conditions that he sees in Asia will only get worse. Although "church history" gives constant testimony to this fact, we need not consult it to document the spiritual decline and captivity of the Body of Christ. One needs only to read II Timothy.

> The character of the last days is strongly marked here, and gives no hope for Christianity as a whole (J.N. Darby).[27]

In II Timothy 3, Paul prophesied that the *"last days"* of the Body of Christ would be *"perilous times"* (3:1), and that *"evil men and seducers shall wax worse and worse, deceiving, and being deceived"* (3:13). As we read :2-4, the correlation between Romans 1 and II Timothy 3 is remarkable. So much so, that one would almost ask Paul, "So, what's new Paul? There is nothing new here, what kind of prophecy is this?"

---

27. J.N. Darby, *Synopsis of the Books of the Bible.*

The difference is this: Romans 1 is a history of the Nations, while II Timothy 3 is a history of "Christendom." No wonder these passages match so well, because the members of the Body of Christ have joined the Gentile world-course, and now they have the character of the world and its religions (*i.e., "the mystery of iniquity"*), instead of having the character of Christ manifested in their lives (*i.e., "the mystery of godliness"*)!

Paul uses the phrase *"perilous times"* to describe the condition of "Christendom." Interestingly, the word translated *"perilous"* is used only one other time. It is found in Matthew 8:28 where it is translated *"fierce,"* and is used in connection with two men who were possessed with devils. Christendom is possessed with the *"doctrines of devils"* just as Paul had warned concerning the *"latter times"* (I Timothy 4:1).

FORM OF GODLINESS

Having a form of godliness, but denying the power thereof:
from such turn away (II Timothy 3:5).

While verses two through four are true of their lives, they attempt
to portray *"a form of godliness"* (:5), and those who lead them
are supposed *"ministers of righteousness"* (II Corinthians 11:15).
Now, we do not mean to imply that every teacher within the
religious system is a satanic minister, for Paul tells us that there
are some vessels unto *"honor"* there (2:20). We appreciate and
honor them – since God does. They are God's dear vessels. Still,
they are unknowingly a part of this satanic *"form"* nonetheless.

The *"form"* of godliness is counterfeit godliness! Strong defines
"form" (#3446) as "appearance." Therefore, the religious
system puts on a good "show"! It is religious show-business; yet
they deny the power of godliness. The source of godliness is our
identification and union in the Lord Jesus Christ – in His death,
burial and resurrection.

For I am not ashamed of the gospel of Christ: for it is the
power of God … (Romans 1:16).

For the preaching of the cross … is the power of God (I
Corinthians 1:18).

… Crucified with Him … (Romans 6:6).

… Buried with Him … (Romans 6:4).

… Raised us up together … (Ephesians 2:6).

… made us sit together in heavenly places in Christ Jesus
(Ephesians 2:6).

I am crucified with Christ; nevertheless I live; yet not I, but

Christ lives in me: and the life that I now live in the flesh I live by the faith of the Son of God, Who loved me, and gave Himself for me (Galatians 2:21).

Now *there's* the power of godliness!

And what is the exceeding greatness of His power toward us who believe, according to the working of His mighty power, which He wrought in Christ, when He raised Him from the dead, and set Him at His Own right hand in heavenly places (Ephesians 1:19-20).

... the power of His resurrection ... (Philippians 3:10).

TURN AWAY

Having a form of godliness, but denying the power thereof:
from such turn away (II Timothy 3:5).

Paul is very clear about what Timothy's response was to be concerning religion, he was to *"turn away"* (II Timothy 3:5), just as the members of the Body of Christ had *"turned away"* (1:15) from Paul. Some might have thought it best to stay in among the religious form, with the hopes of recovering others, but this is human reasoning. The way of divine instruction is to *"turn away."* This phrase *"turn away"* is Paul's sixth such plea for members of Christ's Body to separate from this imitation "church" known as Christendom.

- "Shun" (2:16)
- "Depart" (2:19)
- "Purge" (2:21)
- "Flee" (2:22)
- "Avoid" (2:23)
- "Turn Away" (3:5)

These are all clear words. These are all serious words. Each of us must turn to the Scriptures and answer, by the *context* of II Timothy, the following questions:

From what was the *"iniquity"* which Timothy was to *"depart"*?

What was the *"great house"*?

Who were *"these"* from whom Timothy was to *"purge"* himself?

From what youthful *"lusts"* was Timothy to *"flee"*?

From what were their hearts to be *"pure"*?

From what *"such"* was Timothy to *"turn away"*?

LED AWAY FROM HOME

For of this sort are they who creep into houses, and lead captive silly women laden with sins, led away with diverse lusts (II Timothy 3:6).

Note carefully that the religious system will lead believers *"away."* From where will they be led *"away"*? *"Houses!"* Why would Paul say this? Because the home is the center of all of God's earthly plans and purposes. It always has been *"the church in your house,"* whether God is ministering through Israel or the Body of Christ. Today, the home is the ultimate embodiment of God's church (the *ecclesia*). Thus the Pauline expression, even unto the end of his writings, is that the *ecclesia* is *domestic,* not *institutional.*

It is also important to note the time frame of which Paul speaks. He was speaking of the *"last days"* of the Body of Christ here. Paul is showing us that even unto the *"last days"* the biblical expression of God's *ecclesia* is the home! – and a spiritual warfare surrounds the abandonment of this domestic position – this embassy of heaven.

Why do we say that this is spiritual warfare? Because in the context, saints are being *"led captive"* from *"houses."* They are prisoners of war!

So, Paul describes a wholesale abandonment of *"the church in your house"*[28] in the *"last days."* Thus the saints are being led off to the religious system, where they are kept in bondage.

Interestingly, Paul specifically speaks here of women being *"led away."* Women are especially vulnerable to the subtle pull of the religious system. This is because they are the first line of satanic attack. Consult the story of Eden. It was Eve who was approached by the Adversary and his sermon. The serpent came for the woman – to discuss spiritual matters with her. This is just his modus operandi.

---

28. Not to be confused with the so-called "house church."

LED AWAY WITH DIVERSE LUSTS

For of this sort are they who creep into houses, and lead captive silly women laden with sins, led away with diverse lusts (II Timothy 3:6).

The Adversary accomplishes this captive-leading from the home through religious *"lusts."* They are *"led away with diverse lusts."* We know that these lusts are "religious" because verse six does not end with a period, but with a comma: *"...led away with diverse lusts, ever learning and never able to come to the knowledge of the truth."* The lusts here are for knowledge – religious knowledge.

Does this sound familiar again? Satan came to Eve with the temptation of knowledge from the *"tree of the **knowledge** of good and evil."*

Thus with the husbands' silent abdication of their God given responsibility, the wives are drawn as *"silly"* "groupies" to these organized religious knowledge-fests. Alas, after all their *"learning"* they are *"never able to come to the knowledge of the truth."*

In fact, women are so strongly affected by these lusts, or *passions,* that they become emboldened to disregard the plain teachings of Paul (I Corinthians 14:34-35; I Timothy 2:11-15), and begin taking leadership roles, even teaching the Scriptures themselves in these systems!

THE CREEPERS

For of this sort are they who creep into houses, and lead captive silly women laden with sins, led away with diverse lusts (II Timothy 3:6).

Now, all of this – *leading captive away from the home* – is done in blatant disregard of Paul's teaching, and it is done so under the guise of *"godliness"* (II Timothy 3:5). Just look around at all the "good," "godly," "great" work that is being done "for Christ" in Christendom. This is a *"form,"* an appearance, and things are not always as they appear. That is why those coming into the *"houses"* to lead out the silly (*i.e.,* foolish) women captive are *creepers.*

*For of this sort are they who **creep** into houses …*

The woman is the first target of the satanic attack to lead the church out of its natural habitat – the home – and into the religious system, captive. Therefore, from the satanic viewpoint, the woman is at the heart of the religious system – and her husband, with ring-in-nose, submissively follows suit! Remember the account of Genesis?

*… And **gave also unto her husband with her,** and HE **did** eat* (Genesis 3:6).

The whole system – even when it has male leadership – is designed to be an attack upon the God-ordained role of the head of the home. One brother has well stated, "I am the head of my household in the parking lot, and a child when I walk through the 'church' doors."

We are reminded that "Babylon" is called *"she"* in Revelation chapter 18. It is a feminine system. Remove the woman's presence, work and influence from the system, and it will die.

Perhaps for years, many of us would read verse six and scratch our heads, "What in the world is Paul talking about?" How wonderful context is! For, with context comes the floodlight of understanding, bringing the whole world of religion into focus!

Once again, the indictment in verse six is not so much against "silly women," as it is against their rebellious, lazy and weak heads! It is time for us husbands to stop abdicating the divine responsibility that is ours. It is time to stop voluntarily taking our families "away" to be trained by the Gentile religious system. This is our responsibility, and it is one that cannot be delegated to others. Let's repent of our failure to be the spiritual leaders of our homes. With Bible in hand, let's bring our families back home, leading our wives and children in the Lord's nurture and admonition.

LADEN WITH SINS

*For of this sort are they who creep into houses, and lead captive silly women **laden with sins,** led away with diverse lusts* (II Timothy 3:6).

What is the religious system's power of manipulation over the *"silly* [foolish] *women"* (and men for that matter!)? Guilt – the guilt of heavy-*laden sins.*

The reason that these women are *"foolish"* and can so successfully be *"led away"* is because the religious system has *"laden"* them down *"with sins."* These women are looking to the religious system for a solution to their *guilt* – to cover it, or bury it –when in fact it is the religious system itself that has *"laden"* them with these sins.

Noah Webster[1] defines *"laden"* as "loaded, oppressed and burdened." These women are "loaded with sins;" they are "oppressed with sins;" they are "burdened with sins." They are futilely seeking relief from the very system that was loading them with oppression and burdens.

In fact, the phrase **"laden** *with sins"* could be translated **"buried** *under sins,"* because the word that Paul used was *sōreuō* (*Strong's Greek Lexicon #4987*),

"from another form of 4673," which is *soros.* Interestingly this word means "a funereal receptacle (urn, coffin)."

These women are manipulated by the religious system under such a burden from the guilt of sin that they are *"buried"* beneath it! This has *always* been the greatest tool of religion. Guilt of sin is what keeps people loyal to religion, and religion will always "increase" sin to its highest degree – even to the point of *generating* and *manufacturing* new "sins!"

---

1. Noah Webster, *American Dictionary of the English Language*, 1828.

The Pharisees of Jesus's day were masters of this as well.

For they bind heavy burdens and grievous to be borne, and lay them on men's shoulders; but they themselves will not move them with one of their fingers (Matthew 23:4).

Paul described it this way,

For you suffer, if a man brings you into bondage, if a man devours you, if a man takes of you, if a man exalts himself, if a man smites you on the face (II Corinthians 11:20).

Over the centuries religion, to keep its hold on the masses, has made many more things "sinful" than they really are. By doing so religion keeps increasing the "need" of itself. In fact, if we have had religious influence pressed upon us in our lives, many things that we have known as "sin" may indeed not be so.

Sin, in a biblical sense is that which is an assault against God (*e.g.* worship of other gods, the exaltation of one's self or others equal to or above God), or against man (*i.e.,* that which is harmful or hurtful to others). Religion always seeks to make new lists of "sins,"[2] keeps adding to the "sin catalog." How many things do we regard as "sin" that in all actuality are only the chains of religious bondage? Just because something is said to be a "sin" long and hard enough does not make it a sin.

---

2. I have heard strange lists of "sins" over the years, such as: window-shopping, reading the newspaper, men shaking hands with women, playing cards, playing billiards, going swimming, wearing wire-rim glasses, men parting their hair down the middle, buying gas on Sunday, wearing shorts, chewing gum, watching TV, going to the movies, and wearing cowboy boots; but even some of the more popularly accepted lists of "sins" are to be made subject to the scrutiny of the Word of God.

EVER LEARNING

Ever learning, and never able to come to the knowledge of the truth (II Timothy 3:7).

The religious system sure is impressive. They have their *"form"* (appearance) of godliness, but even though they are *"ever learning,"* they are, indeed, *"never able to come to the knowledge of the truth."*

Just think of all this *"ever learning"* that goes on within the man-made system, of which there seems to be an endless supply:

Sunday School	Bible Seminaries
Sunday morning sermons	Sunday night sermons
Wednesday night Bible studies	Children's churches
Awanas	Daily devotions
New member classes	Summer Bible camps
Revivals	Bible conferences
Seminars	Training programs
Retreats	Christian schools
Bible colleges	Bible Institutes
Daily reading through the Bible in a year	Vacation Bible School

What is the end result for someone in the system, after a lifetime of all this *"ever-learning"*?

– They still do not even know *who they are.*
– They still do not even know *who their Apostle is.*
– They still do not even know *what their message is.*

They cannot carry on a meaningful conversation about justification. As a rule, they still know little more than the Sunday School Bible stories. Something is seriously *wrong,* and what most don't realize is that it is wrong *by design!*

An Imitation

Now as Jannes and Jambres withstood Moses, so do these also resist the truth: men of corrupt minds, reprobate concerning the faith. But they shall proceed no further: for their folly shall be manifest unto all men, as theirs also was (II Timothy 3:8-9).

From the life of Moses, Paul illustrates the point he's making. Jannes and Jambres withstood Moses. Moses, as you know, was God's divinely appointed messenger to Israel. Jannes and Jambres were an imitation of the real thing, even to the point of delusion. So it is with Christendom: it withstands Paul, God's divinely appointed messenger for the Body of Christ. It, too, is an imitation of the real thing. The real thing is the *ecclesia*, the Body of Christ; yet Christendom presents its own versions of "church" to the point of delusion.

God had confrontation with Egypt. On one side was Moses and the testimony of God: on the other side was Pharaoh with his *"wise men," "sorcerers"* and *"magicians."* Pharaoh's ministers *"did in like manner"* as Moses, through the means of their *"enchantments."* They were persuasive imitators.

Nonetheless God has not called us to join the imitation. God has not called us to imitate the religious system – *they* are the imitators! They have the *"form"* of godliness, but without the power. We are the real thing – the mystery of godliness! Don't join the imitators! Be real!

Andre Sneidar has written,

> The church has become (even the early church of Paul's day!) inextricably enmeshed and entangled (*"snare," "taken captive"*) in the tentacles of the religious system (*"great house"* – 2:20).

This is the religious system showing its true colors. In the last days the hallmark of the church will be that it will be so inexorably lost within the grasp of the religious system that there will be a total abandonment of anything to do with God, and with His Apostle to them.

Jannes and Jambres are representative of the religious system of Egypt in Moses' day, and Paul's reference to them here informs us that the same system of mysticism and idolatry held sway in Paul's day, and by current observation, in our day as well.

This is the *"iniquity"* from which the servant of the Lord must *"depart"* (2:19).

The only remedy, the only way to accomplish this, is to LEAVE (*"depart"* – 2:19; see *Thayer*: "… go away … withdraw … flee").

God is calling on the honorable vessels, inviting them to leave the corrupt environment of the sepulcher of dried and empty bones passing itself off as the "real deal" and to which God has said "NO DEAL."

God's calling is *not* to reform "the church," or to improve it in any form or fashion – Paul has made it expressly clear that "the church" will not be the focus of God's effort in the last days. Rather, God's call is to individual men, calling them to LEAVE the corrupt and destitute religious system, and instead take their place in the lonely wilderness outside its confines. This is the way one may become an effective servant.

A PERSECUTION

Yea, and all who will live godly in Christ Jesus shall suffer persecution (II Timothy 3:12).

Paul once again reminds Timothy that things will not be getting any easier. Timothy does not have an easy road ahead. Paul assures Timothy of the results of anyone who determines to live in the fullness of who they are in Christ – *"godly."* This *"godly"* (:12) stands in contrast with the religious system's **"form of godliness"** (:5).

The issue with Paul is not the *appearance* (*i.e.,* form) of godliness. He had that as a Pharisee! This *godly appearance* is an essential part of the religious system! Instead what Paul presents to Timothy is *LIFE!*

*… all who will **live** godly in Christ Jesus …*

This godliness springs forth from LIFE! Where is this life? Those who *"will live godly"* will do so *"in Christ Jesus."* Godliness is being presented here as the life of Christ Jesus in the members of His Body – the *"mystery of godliness"*!

LIVE *in* CHRIST JESUS! *That **is** godliness!*

BEING WHO WE ARE

*Yea, and all who will **live** godly in Christ Jesus shall suffer persecution* (II Timothy 3:12).

We are called to *"live."* We do not need a *"form"* (:5) for we have *"life"* (1:1). We are called simply to *"be"* – to be who and what we are IN CHRIST. We are called just to *"live … in Christ Jesus"* (:12)! We are called to live in our COMPLETENESS in Him (*"… complete in Him …"* – Colossians 2:10). We are called to enjoy HIM as our LIFE! (*"… Christ, Who is our life …"* – Colossians 3:4).

We are not called just to *"live …in Christ Jesus,"* but to *"live **godly** in Christ Jesus."* This word for *"godly"* here is unique. There are only two occurrences of this particular Greek adverb in Scripture. Interestingly enough, they are both from the pen of Paul. The other passage is in Titus (possibly Paul's second to last letter – II Timothy being his last).

*For the grace of God that brings salvation has appeared to all men, teaching us that, denying ungodliness and worldly lusts, we should live soberly, righteously and **godly** in this present world* (Titus 2:11-12).

Paul teaches us here that *grace* is our instructor. Grace is the divinely appointed teacher in this dispensation. No other teacher is *"certified"* (Galatians 1:11-12) – not even the old schoolmaster of the law (Galatians 3:25)!

Notice that there are two parts to the grace curriculum:

… teaching us that, [1] ***denying** … we should* [2] ***live** …*

Denying: The first part of grace's teaching is that of *"denying."* This is, indeed, the first part of the truth of our identification and union with Christ! The meaning of the word *"deny"* is, "to disavow, to renounce." From grace we learn of our position in Christ Jesus, and then we come to a place of agreement (*i.e.*, acknowledgment) with God as to exactly who we are.

What is to be our subsequent response to the old life in Adam? "That's just not me," "That's not who I am," is what we say concerning our former identification. Every believer will either *deny* – day by day, moment by moment – who he **was** in Adam, or who he **is** in Christ!

Live: Paul says, *"we should live."* This is the second part of the truth of our identification and union with Christ! We are *"alive unto God"* (Romans 6:11; Galatians 2:20). The Father desires to manifest (II Corinthians 4:10-11) and magnify (Philippians 1:20) Christ in the members of *the ecclesia* (His Body).

Again, Paul's emphasis is upon us *living*. Grace teaches us to LIVE! – to live to be who and what we are in Christ: *godly!*

It is important to note that, according to the context of II Timothy, this godly life is one that is lived *outside* of the religious system. Just what is the result of such an outsider's life?

> *Yea, and all who will live godly in Christ Jesus shall suffer persecution* (II Timothy 3:12).

Persecution can take many forms, but be assured of this one thing (Paul is *very clear* about this):

ALL WHO **WILL** LIVE GODLY IN CHRIST JESUS **SHALL suffer persecution.**

From where will this persecution come? It will come from the same place it *always* has: **religion!** It is the religious system that always has been at the root of persecution. Don't ever forget that. Religion took Jesus to Calvary, religion stoned Stephen, and religion now had Paul in a Roman prison. History is filled with the zeal of religion's "holy" wars and crusades.

Deny the worldly system of religion, and ***live:*** *"live godly in Christ Jesus"*!

It *is* our calling!

No Need to Look Anywhere Else

But continue in the things which you have learned and have been assured of, knowing of whom you have learned them; and that from a child you have known the holy Scriptures, which are able to make you wise unto salvation through faith which is in Christ Jesus. All Scripture is given by inspiration of God, and is profitable for doctrine, for reproof, for correction, for instruction in righteousness: that the man of God may be perfect, thoroughly furnished unto all good works (II Timothy 3:14-17).

Paul here points Timothy to the Scriptures. This is exactly where he had directed the Ephesian elders as he departed from Asia.

And now, brethren, I commend you to God, and the Word of His grace, which is able to build you up … (Acts 20:32).

Thus we see the all-sufficiency of Scripture. It was all that the elders needed, although they did not avail themselves of it. It was all that Timothy needed. Paul said that it was *able!*

Paul also wrote the Ephesians a letter, after his departure from them, emphasizing the place that the Scriptures had in spiritual warfare.

Take … the sword of the Spirit, which is the Word of God (Ephesians 6:17).

Paul had told Timothy earlier that the Word of God was sufficient for the most constraining situations.

Wherein I suffer trouble, as an evil doer, even unto bonds; but the Word of God is not bound (II Timothy 2:9).

The Source of Profit

In the dark situation in which Timothy found himself, what an encouragement the reminder of these things must have been to him. With only the foundation remaining (II Timothy 2:19), one could easily give up hope. "What's the use?" "The battle's just not worth it!" Still, Paul points Timothy to the place of eternal profit: *"all Scripture … is profitable"* (II Timothy 3:16).

ADULT SONSHIP

That the man of God may be perfect, thoroughly furnished unto all good works (II Timothy 3:17).

Note carefully Paul's usage of the phrase *"the man of God"* in verse 17. He did not say "the child of God," but *"the man of God."* The *"man of God"* is not a clerical term. Paul is *not* talking about clergymen. The word *"man"* here stands in contrast with the word *"child."*

A transition has taken place! No longer children, members of Christ's Body now have been placed into the position and status of full-grown adult sons. This is the glorious doctrine known as *adoption.* This means that the temporary gifts given to the Body of Christ now have been laid aside. The gifts of apostles, prophets, evangelists, pastors and teachers were only temporary *"until"*:

> *until we all come in the unity of the faith, and of the knowledge of the Son of God, unto a perfect man, unto the measure of the stature of the fullness of Christ* (Ephesians 4:13).

One of the characteristic purposes of this *"until"* time is *"that we henceforth be no more children"* (Ephesians 4:14).

We are not just the *"children of God"* – wonderful enough as that is – but we are more than that: through our union with Christ, as members of His body, we're now the *"sons of God."* We are not minor *"children"*; rather, we have the divine position of full-grown sons. This is the position of the Lord Jesus Christ Himself. We have been placed into union with His full adult sonship.

> *To redeem them who were under the law, that we might receive the **adoption of sons*** (Galatians 4:5).

*For you have not received the spirit of bondage again to fear; but you have received the **Spirit of adoption,** whereby we cry, **"Abba, Father"** (Romans 8:15).*

This wonderful reality is often missed because of the more modern usage of the word *"adoption."* We think of taking someone from outside the family and making them a member. This is not the scriptural concept; instead it is that of placement of one into a full-adult *sonship* position.

To live in the establishment of this sonship in our daily lives is to be the mature *"man of God."* What equips the *"man of God"* in his adult function is the proficient Word of God. It enables and empowers the *"man of God"* toward every good work of the Father.

THE SOURCE OF ALL MINISTRY

That the man of God may be perfect, thoroughly furnished unto all good works (II Timothy 3:17).

The *"man of God"* was able, by the Word of God, to be *"thoroughly furnished"* to ***"all*** *good works."* Everything that needed to be accomplished would now be done through the Word of God. The phrase *"thoroughly furnished"* means "to finish out, to equip fully" (Strong's #1822). Though the Body of Christ in its infancy had needed supernatural gifts imparted to them to carry out God's work, the Word of God was now all the equipment that they needed.

> Not one word does Paul say of a successor to his apostleship or of the authority of a church, body of churches, council or creed. The Scriptures, and they alone, are authoritative. (C.I. Scofield)[29]

Our brother Duane Gallentine has some wonderful observations concerning this truth, in his excellent article *He Gave Gifts Unto Men:*

> After the full deposit of *grace truth* was given to Paul, that particular *revelation* called THE MYSTERY, God finalizes the edification process through Scripture. Those men who were once the *"gifts unto men"* were diminishing. II Timothy 3:16-17 reveals that the … ministry of the gifted men had been replaced with Scriptures that do the very same thing, God replacing their … ministry … with His Word of Truth found in a Book … God's full complete Word in the Bible.
>
> With the Epistle of Second Timothy being the last book in the Bible to be written, while Paul was near his execution, God had used His internal "gift system" to copy, collect

---

29. C.I. Scofield, *The Scofield Bible Correspondence Course,* (Moody Bible Institute, 1960) Volume IV, Epistles and Revelation, page 870.

and collate all which is Scripture. The Body of Christ, the church of the living God, was the pillar and the ground of the truth (I Timothy 3:15). God's design was to have all Scripture resident within the Body of Christ before Paul

died, with his Second Epistle to Timothy concluding that deposit of Truth. We have sixty-six books of Scripture found in a *one-volume* book. These are the Writings that God breathed, called Scripture (II Timothy 3:16-17; Romans 16:25-26; I Corinthians 14:37; Colossians 4:16).

Since the death of Paul, the Apostle, God's edifying process for giving *doctrine, reproof, correction and instruction in righteousness* to the saints has been through the Bible, NOT a man in a ministry, for *that* is not the means as stated in II Timothy 3:16. Through the Word of Truth found in a BOOK studied "rightly divided" we grow up IN CHRIST and become workmen of God (Ephesians 4:15; II Timothy 2:15).[30]

---

30. Duane Gallentine, *He Gave Gifts Unto Men,* Bible Student's Press,™ 1992.

II Timothy Chapter 4

THEY WILL NOT ENDURE SOUND DOCTRINE

For the time will come when they will not endure sound doctrine; but after their own lusts shall they heap to themselves teachers, having itching ears (II Timothy 4:3).

Paul once again tells Timothy that things are only going to get worse. Those who once held and embraced Paul's special revelation would no longer endure it being taught. It is not that they would not endure teaching: they just would not endure *sound* teaching – they would only go so far!

Paul was not guessing here. Notice how clearly he states this, *"For the time **will** come when they will not endure sound doctrine."* This is a part of Paul's continuing prophecy of the future condition of the church, which is His Body, and it would find fulfillment in Timothy's lifetime.

To satisfy their appetites for *unsound* doctrine, they *"after their own lusts shall heap to themselves teachers, having itching ears."*

A Heap Pile of Teachers

[They] shall invite teachers *en masse*. In periods of unsettled faith … teachers of all kinds swarm like the flies of Egypt. The demand creates the supply. The hearers invite and shape their own preachers. If the people desire a calf to worship, a ministerial calf-maker is readily found.[31]

So it is in our day. Could there ever have been a greater *heap pile* of teachers than today? Christendom is buried under such

---

31. Martin R. Vincent, *Word Studies in the New Testament*, Volume IV, pages 320-321.

a heap, and the Body of Christ with it! We have a saturation of such teaching – teaching that does not suit this *"dispensation of the grace of God"* committed to Paul. It is everywhere. Endless religious radio and television broadcasts fill the air waves 24 hours a day. We have an incomprehensible *heap pile* of teaching through: books, booklets, pamphlets, tracts, study guides, magazines, journals, audio cassettes, video tapes, creeds, confessions, articles of faith, doctrinal statements, "churches," "fellowships," "ministries," centers, schools, colleges, Bible institutes, seminaries, Sunday schools, and now through the world wide web. Has the Body of Christ ever had such a *heap pile* of unsound teaching – teaching that has abandoned Paul's distinct revelation to the Body of Christ? We are drowning in it! There is every color, size, flavor and style of teaching to suit anyone's fancy (*"itching ears"*).

TURNED AWAY THEIR EARS FROM THE TRUTH AND TURNED UNTO FABLES

And they shall turn away their ears from the truth, and shall be turned unto fables (II Timothy 4:4).

Paul knew and foretold of the time when the Body of Christ (as a whole) would abandon *the truth* (as a whole). They would *"turn away"* just as all those in Asia had done (II Timothy 1:15). The Asian ministry was the foretaste and model of the future! They would endure *any* and *all* teaching, EXCEPT the truth!

The result of all of this is that the Body of Christ lives in fantasy and superstition. We have been *"turned unto fables."* The Body of Christ now has been MYTH-taken. This is the sad commentary of modern-day Christendom! We have lost our scriptural bearing from the flood of *unsound* teaching.

> The root of the apostasy of the church is their having *"turned away"* from Paul and his *"form of sound words"* (1:15, 13). They were turned *"away … from the truth … unto fables"* (4:4). (Andre Sneidar)

As real as these threats were to the believer of Paul's day, two thousand years have added a thick maze of twisted tales masquerading as the truth. The result has been that the overwhelming majority of Christendom finds itself being *myth-taken*. They are buried deep in the darkness of a "Christian" mythology.

It is no small task for the student of Scripture to study and sort through traditional "Christian" mythology and the actual truth of the Bible; but it is a noble and rewarding journey. It requires diligent and faithful dedication to the actual words of God. The saints at Berea modeled this spirit of loyalty to what God had said:

These were more noble than those in Thessalonica, in that they received the word with all readiness of mind, and searched the Scriptures daily, whether those things were so (Acts 17:11).

What a life-long task every workman of the Scriptures has. It involves never allowing ourselves to be locked into *any* man-made creed or systematic theology; while cultivating an ever-adjusting heart and mind to what has been learned afresh from the Scriptures. It requires an attitude and spirit of adjustableness.

Study to show yourself approved unto God, a workman that needs not to be ashamed, rightly dividing the Word of Truth (II Timothy 2:15).

Paul calls us *out* of all of this mess. He calls us simply to *stand fast* in the liberty (Galatians 5:1), grace (Romans 5:2) and simplicity that are in Christ (II Corinthians 11:3) – having done all to *stand* (Ephesians 6:13)!

Do not spend your life following the fables of Christendom, being *myth-taken*. Join the noble sons of God who are diligently searching the Scriptures to see if those things are so. Be *truth-taken!*

Abandon the *heap pile* and stand *outside* with Christ!

DO THE WORK OF AN EVANGELIST

*But watch in all things, endure afflictions, **do the work of an evangelist,** make full proof of your ministry* (II Timothy 4:5).

Evangelism was one of the ascension gifts. The purpose of these special ascension gifts was *"for the perfecting of the saints, for the work of the ministry, for the edifying of the body of Christ"* (Ephesians 4:12) – all in lieu of the fact that they did not yet have the full, complete revelation of God in written form.

Now, as Paul writes his final epistle, all these things – *"the perfecting of the saints," "the work of the ministry" and "the edifying of the body of Christ"* – take place by the application of the full (*i.e.,* complete), written Word of God, finished by the hand of Paul. No "gifts" are now needed. There are no divine/ supernatural gifts of apostle, prophet, evangelist, pastor or teacher today.

Someone may carry out certain aspects of these – such as evangelist or teacher – but they do so not by these special gifts, but by dedication to the written Word of God. If a man will teach, for example, he must labor in the study of the Word – learning, adjusting, growing – so that he may teach others. It is not a "gift" in any sense of the ascension gifts.

This is why Paul told Timothy to **"do** *the work of an evangelist."*

Paul does not tell Timothy that he has the "gift" of "evangelist." Nor does he say that he is "an evangelist." He only tells him to do an evangelist's work – *"do the work of an evangelist."* He could now do so – without the divine "gifts" of the ascension – because he had in his possession the full, complete Scripture which was ABLE to ENABLE him to *"do the work of an evangelist"* thus making *"full proof"* of his ministry.

"Gifts" were no longer needed. The Scriptures themselves – now full and complete – were *"profitable"* for *"doctrine [i.e., teaching],"* etc. ... *"that the man of God may be perfect, thoroughly furnished unto all good works"* (II Timothy 3:17).

Notice again the results: *"that the man of God may be ..."* – what? – *"perfect, thoroughly furnished."* That's what the full, complete Scriptures can do! For what purpose? *"Unto all good works."* This is why Paul tells Timothy to *"do the work of an evangelist."*

A LONELY STAND

For Demas has forsaken me, having loved this present world, and is departed unto Thessalonica; Crescens to Galatia, Titus unto Dalmatia. Only Luke is with me … (II Timothy 4:10-11).

Timothy and Paul had lonely stands. Timothy was in Asia where all had turned away from Paul (II Timothy 1:15). Paul was in Rome where *"only Luke"* (II Timothy 4:11) was with him.

Demas (as well as Crescens and Titus, it would appear) forsook Paul, *"having loved this present world"* (II Timothy 4:10). Does this mean that they forsook Paul for what is often viewed as "worldliness?" What was it about this present age that made them forsake Paul? The context of the entire book of II Timothy would seem to indicate that this was the abandonment of Paul for this present *religious* age. Theirs was a wholesale abandonment for this world's *religious* course.

The Faithful Five

Five men are specifically listed by name who had remained faithful. You could count them on one hand. There was of course Paul, and Luke who was with him (II Timothy 4:11). Then there was Timothy, and Mark who was with him (II Timothy 4:11); and there is Tychicus (II Timothy 4:12).

The situation was so bleak that when Paul first appeared on trial before the authorities not a single soul stood with him. He stood on trial all alone. *"At my first answer no man stood with me, but all men forsook me: I pray God that it may not be laid to their charge"* (II Timothy 4:16).

STANDING ALONE

Paul was not the first of God's servants to stand alone. M.H. Reynolds[32] has written movingly regarding this crucial point:

It is human to stand with the crowd, it is divine to stand alone. It is man-like to follow the people, to drift with the tide; it is God-like to follow a principle, to stem the tide.

It is natural to compromise conscience and follow the social and religious fashion for the sake of gain or pleasure; it is divine to sacrifice both on the altar of truth and duty.

"No man stood with me, but all men forsook me" (II Timothy 4:16), wrote the battle-scarred apostle in describing his first appearance before Nero to answer for his life of believing and teaching contrary to the Roman world.

Truth has been out of fashion since man changed his robe of fadeless light for a garment of faded leaves. Noah built and voyaged **alone.** Daniel dined and prayed **alone.** Elijah sacrificed and witnessed **alone.** Jeremiah prophesied and wept **alone.** Jesus loved and died **alone**.

The church in the wilderness praised Abraham and persecuted Moses. The church of kings praised Moses and persecuted the prophets. The church of Caiaphas praised the prophets and persecuted Jesus. The church of the popes praised the Savior and persecuted the saints. And multitudes now, both in the church and the world, applaud the courage and fortitude of the patriarchs and prophets, the apostles and martyrs, but condemn as stubbornness or foolishness the same faithfulness to truth today.

Wanted, today, men and women, young and old, who

32. Marion H. Reynolds, Jr. (1919 -1997), Standing Alone, *Foundation Magazine.*

will obey their conviction of truth and duty at the cost of fortune, friends and life itself.

Wherefore Jesus also, that He might sanctify the people with His Own blood, suffered without the gate. Let us go forth therefore unto Him without the camp, bearing His reproach (Hebrews 13:12-13).

NOT SO LONELY AFTER ALL

Notwithstanding the Lord stood with me, and strengthened me; that by me the preaching might be fully known, and that all the Gentiles might hear ... (II Timothy 4:17).

That no one stood with Paul when he faced his trial is only part of the story! The fact is, Paul *did* have someone who stood with him while he was on trial – THE LORD!

If we look to men we will surely be disappointed; but if we keep our eyes on the Lord, we will always find strength. He is the One Who bears the name "FAITHFUL AND TRUE!"

*And I saw heaven opened, and behold a white horse; and He Who sat upon him was called **Faithful and True** ... (Revelation 19:11).*

This all reminds us of the promise that had been made to Israel of old.

Fear not; for I am with you: be not dismayed; for I am your God: I will strengthen you; yea, I will help you; yea, I will uphold you with the right hand of My righteousness (Isaiah 41:10).

Yet another wonderful promise is made to the Hebrews:

... I will never leave you, nor forsake you (Hebrews 13:5).

Of course there are Paul's grand words to the Ephesians,

Finally, my brothers, be strong in the Lord, and in the power of His might (Ephesians 6:10).

LONELY, BUT NEVER ALONE

Notwithstanding the Lord stood with me, and strengthened me; that by me the preaching might be fully known, and that all the Gentiles might hear … (II Timothy 4:17).

Another brother touchingly writes on this important theme.

There are many in the Body of Christ who are in transition between "going" to church and "being" the Church … The more in tune with the Lord we become, the more dissatisfied and uncomfortable we become with what is being said and done in His Name. Yet, there is an uncomfortable pause between where we used to be and where we are called to be. It is a lonely time in which we will be misunderstood by many that have not seen what we have seen.

What God is impressing upon many of us who are in-between the church as a building and the church as a lifestyle is how to walk ALONE … God would have us learn to fellowship with Christ, even if it means to take the lonely path.

Many times the desire to find other "like-minded believers" is not a spiritual desire. It is rather our emotion, which longs to be with people who understand us … [Yet we] must know Christ as Fellowship. Abiding in Him, connected to the Head, [we] maintain oneness with the rest of the Body …

Some are able to maintain a sweet spirit so long as they are in fellowship with other believers. But when God allows that fellowship to be interrupted, observe how quickly that sweet spirit turns sour. They will even acknowledge their poor state and say things like, "My temper has become awful. It is because I have been out of church. I must go back this Sunday." Then they will go back to "church," feel uplifted, and the sweet spirit returns. Sadly, this is the experience of a majority of people who have not learned to take Christ as their Life. Is this walking in the Spirit? It is not …

Let us remember that Christ's Body is a spiritual Body. Being in the physical presence of other members does not make us more of a member, and being removed from the physical presence of other members does not make us any less a member. Of course, the exact opposite is true for those meeting together as an institution: without their physical presence and support they lose place as a member; but not so with Christ's Body, the Church. We are not more or less of a member by reason of our physical contact or lack of physical contact with one another.

We may thirst for fellowship not so much to edify the Body as to be edified ourselves – a mindset carried over from when we used to "go to church" to "be fed" once or twice a week. If this is the case, it is no wonder that God would have us look to Him alone as our edification and learn to draw upon Him before placing us in close proximity with others. One weakness of the institutional "church" is that the majority of members are coming to receive, to be edified, to be encouraged, to be fed. It is all "take," and very little "give." Hence, there is little Life …

Let us press into Christ with all our heart, and not be discouraged if we find ourselves temporarily without the fellowship and comfort of our brothers and sisters. Though we are lonely, we are never alone.[33]

---

33. Chip Brogden, *Bible Student's Notebook*, Vol. 7 No. 161.

Postscript

SUFFERING IN THE LAST DAYS

We will conclude these brief comments on II Timothy with these words from A.E. Knoch, from his outstanding work *The Problem of Evil*:

> Paul's second epistle to Timothy is concerned with the last days, so it applies to us in a very special way, for it is adapted to the conditions under which we live. It is the most perilous period in this administration. The truth is being withstood as never before. Sound teaching is not tolerated and many are turned aside to myths. Disorder is everywhere. Insubjection is rampant and even disguises itself as submission to the Lord. Yet the trials of the time give us an opportunity to endure suffering and shame, which will win a rich reward at the dais [the Judgment Seat of Christ].
>
> In some respects it is more difficult to avoid suffering in these last days than in Timothy's time. The Scriptures declare that, in these days, men will be selfish, fond of money, ostentatious, proud, calumniators, stubborn to parents, ungrateful, malign, without natural affection, implacable, adversaries, uncontrollable, fierce, averse to the good, traitors, rash, conceited, fond of their own gratification rather than fond of God, having a form of devoutness, yet denying its power – such we are bidden to shun (II Timothy 3:1-5). Is it possible to live amongst such "saints" and not suffer? Thank God, the Scriptures do not say that *all* are to be like this, nor does each one have all of these traits, but we cannot help suffering from their very presence. Until we become acquainted with them we may not even know that they are included in this list. Some sins, such as selfishness, are so prevalent, that they do not impress us at first. Yet it behooves

each one of us to be aware of this word, and to watch that we are not even tinged with such sins.

Few of the saints seem to be aware of the stratagems of the Adversary and the pain inflicted by his fiery arrows in case we are not shielded by faith. If they were more alive to the opposition of the world-mights of this darkness (Ephesians 6:11-17), they would not so readily yield themselves to their designs and become his tools in opposing those who are standing in the breach for the celestial truths against which the enemy is arrayed.

Whatever our lot, we can be assured with Paul of our Lord's rescue in that day *"from every wicked work."* He will indeed save His Own for His celestial kingdom, *"to Whom be glory for the eons of the eons. Amen!"* (II Timothy 4:18).

May we have grace to take advantage of our special privileges, and use them to glorify His Name!

II Timothy
(A Bible Student's Version[1])

1 Paul, Jesus Christ's apostle by God's will, for the proclamation of life which is in Christ Jesus,

[2] To Timothy, my dearly beloved son: Grace, mercy, and peace, from God our Father and Christ Jesus our Lord.

[3] I thank God, Whom I worship from my forefathers in pure conscience, that I constantly remember you in my prayers night and day;

[4] Longing to see you, remembering your tears, so that I may be filled with joy;

[5] Recalling the sincere faith that is in you, which first made its home in your grandmother Lois, and your mother Eunice; and I am confident it is also in you.

[6] For this reason remember to strengthen God's gift, which is in you by the laying on of my hands.

[7] Because God has not given us a spirit of fear, but of power, love and sober-mindedness.

[8] Don't be ashamed of the testimony of our Lord, nor of me His prisoner: instead, suffer evil with me for the good news, by God's power;

[9] Who saved us, and called us with a holy calling, not according to our performance, but according to His Own purpose and grace, which was given to us in Christ Jesus before the ages began;

[10] But is now made known by the advent of our Savior Jesus Christ, in that He has abolished death, and has illuminated life and incorruption through the good news:

[11] To which I was appointed a proclaimer, and an apostle, and a teacher of the nations.

[12] Because of this I also suffer these things: But I am not ashamed: because I know Whom I have believed, and am sure that He is able to protect what I have entrusted to Him

---

1. A *Bible Student's Version* is our own "version" of the text to assist us in the accuracy, clarity, simplicity and crystallization of our own personal studies.

until that day.

¹³ Hold to the pattern of sound words, which you have heard from me, in faith and love which is in Christ Jesus.

¹⁴ Protect the noble deposit which was entrusted to you, by the Holy Spirit which lives in us.

¹⁵ This you know, that all those who are in Asia turned away from me; including Phygellus and Hermogenes.

¹⁶ The Lord grant mercy to Onesiphorus's family; because he often refreshed me, and was not ashamed of my imprisonment:

¹⁷ But, when he was in Rome, he diligently searched for me, and found me.

¹⁸ The Lord grant that he may find mercy in that day: and you know very well how much he ministered to me at Ephesus.

2 Therefore, my son, be strong in the grace that is in Christ Jesus.

² And what you have heard from me through many witnesses, these entrust to faithful men, who will be competent to teach others also.

³ Therefore suffer evil with me, as Jesus Christ's noble soldier.

⁴ No one serving as a soldier entangles himself with the affairs of this life; so that he may please the one who enlisted him to be a soldier.

⁵ And if a man also competes in games, yet he is not crowned, except he competes according to the rules.

⁶ The farmer must work first, and then partake of his crops.

⁷ Consider what I say; and the Lord will give you understanding in all things.

⁸ Remember that Jesus Christ, David's descendant, was raised from among the dead according to my good news:

⁹ For which I suffer evil, as a criminal, even to imprisonment; but God's Word is not imprisoned.

¹⁰ For this reason I endure all things for the sake of the chosen ones, that they also may obtain the salvation which is in Christ Jesus with age-abiding glory.

¹¹ It is a sure saying: For if we died with Him, we will also live together with Him:

¹² If we endure patiently, we will also reign together with Him: if we deny Him, He also will deny us:

¹³ If we believe not, yet He abides faithful: for He cannot deny Himself.

¹⁴ Remind them of these things, charging them before the Lord that they contend not about words to no value, but to the overthrowing of the hearers.

¹⁵ Study to show yourself approved to God, an unashamed worker, rightly dividing the Word of Truth.

¹⁶ But avoid hostile and pointless discussions: because they will increase to more ungodliness.

¹⁷ And their word will eat as does gangrene: of whom is Hymenaeus and Philetus;

¹⁸ For they have erred concerning the truth, saying that the resurrection has taken place; and overthrow the faith of some.

¹⁹ However God's firm foundation stands solid, having this seal, "The Lord knows those who are His." And, "Let every one who names Christ's name withdraw from injustice."

²⁰ But in a large house there are not only gold and silver vessels, but also wood and clay; some are indeed for special use, and some for ordinary.

²¹ If a man therefore will cleanse himself from among these, he will be a special vessel, sanctified and for the owner's noble use, and prepared to every good work.

²² Flee also the youthful desires: but follow rightness, faith, love, peace, with those who call on the Lord out of a pure heart.

²³ But avoid the foolish and ignorant questions, knowing that they breed contentions.

²⁴ And the Lord's servant must not be contentious; but be gentle to all men, instructive, patient, enduring under evil,

²⁵ Educating the opposition in meekness; if perhaps God will grant them a change of mind to the recognition of the truth:

²⁶ And that sobering up, they may untangle themselves out

of the Adversary's trap, who are taken captive by him for his pleasure.

3 Of this take note, that in the last days difficult seasons will come.
² Because men will be selfish, greedy, arrogant, proud, slanderous, disobedient to parents, ungrateful, unholy,
³ Without family affection, deceitful, adversarial, uncontrollable, inhuman, despisers of good men,
⁴ Traitors, headstrong, conceited, pleasure lovers more than God lovers;
⁵ Having an appearance of godliness, but denying its power: avoid these.
⁶ These are those who sneak into homes, and capture foolish women buried under sins, led away by various passions;
⁷ Always learning, and never able to come to the recognition of the truth.
⁸ Now as Jannes and Jambres opposed Moses, so do these also oppose the truth: men of corrupt minds, worthless concerning the faith.
⁹ But they will not advance any further: because their madness will become obvious to all men, as theirs also was.
¹⁰ But you have closely studied my teaching, conduct, purpose, faith, long-suffering, love, patience,
¹¹ Persecutions, hardships, that came to me in Antioch, at Iconium, at Lystra; what persecutions I endured! But through them all the Lord delivered me.
¹² And all who desire to live godly in Christ Jesus will be persecuted.
¹³ But evil men and imposters will become worse and worse, deceiving, and being deceived.
¹⁴ But continue in what you have learned and been entrusted with, knowing from whom you learned them;
¹⁵ And that from a child you have known the holy Scriptures, which are able to make you wise to salvation through faith which is in Christ Jesus.
¹⁶ All Scripture is God-breathed, and is beneficial for teaching,

for evidence, for correction, for education in rightness:

[17] So that God's man may be complete, fully equipped for every noble work.

4 I summon you therefore before God, and the Lord Jesus Christ, Who will judge the living and the dead at His advent and His kingdom;

[2] Proclaim the Word; stand upon it, conveniently and inconveniently; convince, warn, encourage with all patience and instruction.

[3] Because the season will come when they will not tolerate the sound teaching; but after their own desires will they multiply to themselves teachers that they are itching to hear;

[4] And they will turn away their hearing from the truth, and will be turned to myths.

[5] But be on guard in all things, suffer evil, do the work of an evangelist, fully discharge your ministry.

[6] For I am already being poured out as a drink-offering, and the time of my departure is near.

[7] I have fought the noble fight, I have finished the race, I have protected the faith:

[8] Furthermore there is reserved for me the crown of righteousness, which the Lord, the just Judge, will award me at that day: and not only to me, but to all them also who love His advent.

[9] Try to come to me quickly:

[10] For Demas has deserted me, loving this present age, and has gone to Thessalonica; Crescens to Galatia, Titus to Dalmatia.

[11] Only Luke is with me. Pick up Mark and bring him back with you: because he is valuable for my ministry.

[12] And Tychicus I sent to Ephesus.

[13] When you come bring the overcoat that I left in Troas with Carpus, and the books, but especially the writing-paper.

[14] Alexander the coppersmith did many evil things against me: the Lord will reward him according to his actions:

[15] Beware of him; because he has strongly opposed our words.

[16] At my first defense no one stood by me, but all men deserted me: don't hold it against them.

[17] Yet, the Lord stood with me, and strengthened me; so that by me the proclamation might be fully established, that all nations might hear: and I was delivered from the lion's mouth.

[18] And the Lord will deliver me from every evil design, and will preserve me to His heavenly kingdom; to Whom be glory for ages of ages. Amen.

[19] Give my regards to Priscilla and Aquila, and Onesiphorus' family.

[20] Erastus stayed at Corinth: but I left Trophimus in Miletum sick.

[21] Try to come before winter. Eubulus sends regards to you, and Pudens, and Linus, and Claudia, and all the brothers.

[22] The Lord Jesus Christ be with your spirit. Grace be with you. Amen.

BIBLIOGRAPHY

Allen, Stuart, *Letters From Prison,* Berean Publishing Trust, 1965

Anderson, Sir Robert (1841-1918), *The Buddha of Christendom,* Hodder & Stoughton, 1899

Arndt and Gingrich's *Greek-English Lexicon,* University of Chicago Press, 1952

Brogden, Chip, cited in *Bible Student's Notebook*, Vol. 7 No. 161

Bullinger, E.W. (1837-1913), *The Companion Bible,* Kregel Publications

Darby, J.N. (1800-1882), *The Synopsis of the Books of the Bible,* Bible Truth Depot

Gallentine, Duane, *He Gave Gifts Unto Men,* Bible Student's Press

Hole, F.B., *Paul's Epistles,* Central Bible Hammond Trust

Knoch, A.E. (1874-1965), *The Problem of Evil,* Concordant Publishing Concern, 2008

McCroskey, D.L. (1902-1991), *II Timothy: The Divine Outline of World Apostasy*, Last Day Messenger, Nov.-Dec., 1975

Reynolds, Jr., Marion H. (1919-1997), Standing Alone, *Foundation Magazine*

Scofield, C.I. (1843-1921), *Scofield Reference Bible,* Oxford Press

_____, *The Scofield Bible Correspondence Course,* Moody Bible Institute, 1960

Stam, C.R. (1909-2003), *The Pastoral Epistles*, Berean Bible Society

Strong, James, *The Exhaustive Concordance of the Bible*

Thayer, Joseph H., *Thayer's Greek-English Lexicon of the New Testament;* Baker, Grand Rapids (1995)

Vincent, Martin R., *Word Studies in the New Testament,* 1886

Welch, Charles (1888-1967), *The Berean Expositor XXXI,* Berean Publishing Trust

Williams, George (1850-1928), *Student's Commentary on the Holy Scriptures,* Kregel Publications

Suggested Reading
on Paul's Gospel (Evangel)

The Church Epistles by E.W. Bullinger. Bullinger defends Paul's epistles as God's unique revelation, expounding the great truth of the mystery, the Body of Christ. In this volume he focuses on Paul's letters written to the churches.

God's Eonian Purpose by Adlai Loudy. This work is a thorough review of God's plan and purpose, gathering together many of the most basic themes of Scripture, including *The Beginning of Creation, The Eons and Administrations, Justification, The Conciliation, Completeness in Christ*, and *The Goal of the Universe*. These and other vital subjects are presented in an interesting and informative manner which will appeal to the sincere student of Scripture for the strengthening of faith. The book contains charts and illustrations which provide a welcome visual supplement to the text. We live in a day when few believers have a good grasp of the truth that God has a purpose. Many reason that as long as they themselves are saved, nothing else really matters; but to know Christ and to rejoice in the glory of God is just as important. We need to listen to His Word and receive the glorious revelations He has made concerning His operations and goal if we are to possess real joy and satisfying peace.

The Gospel of Our Salvation by Adlai Loudy. This book explores the various gospels of the Scripture, with a special emphasis given to the message of God's grace for believers today.

The Mystery: Secret Truth Revealed by E.W. Bullinger. There is no subject of greater importance to the Church than that which is called "The Mystery." 5 Mysteries are carefully considered with significance being placed upon the "Great" secret concerning "the Body of Christ."

The Mystery of the Gospel by A.E. Knoch. The "*mysteries*" in God's Holy Word are simply secrets. Once they were hidden and could not be known. When Paul, the apostle to the gentiles, was held captive in Rome, his burning desire was to blaze abroad the Secret. No longer could he go among the *ecclesias* to impart God's glorious revelation, so in Ephesians 6:19 he asked his readers to pray for him that he might open his mouth with boldness *"to make known the secret of the evangel."*

The Revelation of the Mystery by Robert C. Brock. A booklet providing an overview of the mystery revelation committed to Paul, the Apostle.

To Enlighten All as to the Secret by A.E. Knoch. The letter to the Ephesians is an elaboration of the definition of the present secret economy of which Paul became the dispenser.

Why Paul? by A.A. Sandoz. A 25 point Bible study out-line setting forth Paul's distinctive heavenly calling and ministry. Unveiling practical truth veiled by traditions.

All of these are available from:
StudyShelf.com
1-800-784-6010

ENJOY BOOKS?

Visit us at:

www.StudyShelf.com

Over the years we have often been asked to recommend books. The requests come from believers who longed for material with substance. Study Shelf™ is a collection of books which are, in our opinion, the very best in print. Many of these books are "unknown" to the members of the Body of Christ at large, and most are not available at your local "Christian" bookstore.

YOU CAN:

Read

A wealth of articles from past issues of the *Bible Student's Notebook* ™

Purchase

Rare and hard to find books, booklets, leaflets, Bibles, etc. in our 24/7 online store.

Do You Subscribe to the Bible Student's Notebook™?

This is a periodical that ...

- Promotes the study of the Bible.
- Encourages the growth of the believer in grace.
- Supports the role of the family patriarch.
- Is dedicated to the recovery of truth that h a s too long been hidden under the veils of tradition-alism, prejudice, misunderstanding and fear.
- Is not connected with any "Movement," "Organization," "Mission," or separate body of believers, but is sent forth to and for all saints.

The *Bible Student's Notebook*™ is published weekly.

SUBSCRIBE TODAY!

<u>Electronic Version</u> (e-mailed to you)

1 Year – *52 issues* *$10*
2 Years – *104 Issues* *$20*

<u>Printed Version</u> (mailed to you)

½ Year – *26 Issues* *$25*
1 Year – *52 Issues* *$50*

***Bible Student's Notebook*™**
PO Box 265 Windber, PA 15963
www.BibleStudentsNotebook.com
1-800-784-6010

DAILY EMAIL GOODIES™

Do you receive our
Daily Email Goodies™?

These are free daily emails that contain short quotes, articles, and studies on Biblical themes.

These are the original writings of Clyde L. Pilkington, Jr, as well as gleanings from other authors.

<u>Here is what our readers are saying</u>:

"Profound! Comforting! Calming! Wonderful!" – NC

"The Daily Email Goodies continue to bless my heart! ... They provide plenty of food for thought." – IL

"I really appreciate the Goodies!" – VA

"Your Daily Email Goodies are making me aware of authors whose names I don't even know." – GA

"I am glad to be getting the Daily Email Goodies – keep 'em coming." – IN

Request to be added to our free
Daily Email Goodies™

If you would like to be added to the mailing list, email us at:
Goodies@StudyShelf.com

Believer's Warfare, The: Wearing the Armor of Light in the Darkness of this World

(#7000) The believer is in the middle of an ancient spiritual warfare that is as old as mankind. The battle itself, although intense, is not complicated. It is not a process of spiritual hoop-jumping. Indeed it is simple. The Believer's Warfare surveys a few key passages of Scripture to reveal God's sure plan of victory in the life of His saints. ISBN: 9781934251003 – 48 pages, BK.

Bible Student's Notebook, The (VOLUMES)

The Bible Student's Notebook is a periodical dedicated to the: - Promotion of Bible study - Encouragement of the believer's growth in grace - Support of the role of family patriarch - Recovery of truth that has too long been hidden under the veils of traditionalism, prejudice, misunderstanding and fear. The Bible Student's Notebook is not connected with any "Church," "Movement," "Organization," "Society," "Mission," or separate body of believers, but is sent forth to and for all of God's saints. Available in Paperback Volumes.

Church in Ruins, The: Brief Thoughts on II Timothy

(#3325) This brief survey of Paul's last epistle will reveal that, while almost 2000 years have transpired, the condition of the church has remained the same, and indeed has worsened in accordance with Paul's warning to Timothy. This book is not a call for a re-awakening of "the church," because it is apparent that this is not Father's plan. Rather, it is a call to individual men – men whose place in the Christian religious system has left them empty, stagnant and restless – to awaken to Father's call to be His faithful servant and stand outside of that system to look for other faithful men as well. – 128 pages, PB.

Due Benevolence: A Study of Biblical Sexuality

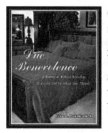 (#3775) Think you have read all that there is on the subject of sexuality from the Bible? Think again! Religious moralist have taken the wonderful gifts of human beauty and sexuality, and made them something dirty and sinful. Much is at stake regarding truth, as well as the nature and character of God Himself. A groundbreaking work providing:

- A refreshingly honest and uninhibited look at sexuality.
- A breath of fresh air from the religious and Victorian mentality.
- A daring and valuable glimpse at the wonderful light just outside sexuality's prison-cell door.

– 220 pages, PB.

Heaven's Embassy: The Divine Plan & Purpose of the Home

(#5675) The home is central to all of God's dealings with man throughout the course of time. It is His Divine "institution" and "organization" upon the earth, and for the believer, it is the Embassy of Heaven. An embassy is "the residence or office of an ambassador." Since the believer is an ambassador of the Lord Jesus Christ (II Corinthians 5:14-21), his home is thus the Divine Embassy of heavenly ministry. Pauline ministry is centered in the homes of believers. This is even the 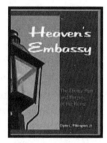 true sphere of the Body of Christ; for this reason our apostle speaks of "church in thy house." This book doesn't focus upon the external specifics of the ministry of Heaven's Embassy (such as hospitality); that will be saved for another volume. Instead, it looks at the inner-workings of the Embassy itself; focusing upon its very nature and internal purpose and function. – 250 pages, PB.

I Choose! Living Life to Its Fullest

 (#4120) Forty-Eight Daily Thoughts on Divine Life. You are alive! Yet not just alive, but alive with the very life of God! Don't allow your "What if …" imaginations of the past or the future to lay claim to the present that God has given you. Allow the objective, unchanging truth of who God has made you in the Lord Jesus Christ to transform your mind and life as you take this spiritual journey of "I Choose." – 192 pages, PB.

Nothing Will Be Lost! The Truth About God's Good News

(#3750) This is an abridgement of the larger work The Salvation of All. It is designed as a give-away edition, with quantity pricing available. – 88 pages, PB.

The Outsiders: God's Called-Out Ones – A Biblical Look at the Church – God's Ecclesia

(#4125) In 1995, after sixteen years of being in the "pastorate" the author walked away. He left the "religious system" by resigning from the very "church" and "ministry" he had formed. In many ways this work is a testament to these actions. This testimony was thirty years in the making – the results of a spiritual journey that the author found to be common to other saints scattered throughout the world and across history. This is an opportunity to explain why some who love the Lord no longer "go to church." It does not seek to persuade  others to do something different; but rather to be simply who and what they already are "in Him." This is an uncovering of the truth of the church, and an encouragement for the members of His Body to enjoy the position and standing "in Christ" that they already possess, realizing that they are truly *"complete in Him"* (Colossians 2:10), that He alone is their Life (Colossians 3:4), and that His Life is full of freedom (Galatians 5:1). ISBN: 9781934251614 – 128 pages, PB.

Plowboy's Bible, The : God's Word for Common Man

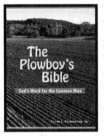

(#4425) Shocking conclusions from the man that brought you The King James Bible Song. This book represents years of study and a significant change in understanding. Raised on and trained in a "King James Only" position, most of the author's teaching ministry was centered on the defense of the KJV. He had early associations with major proponents of this position and their followers. He actively taught classes and seminars on the subject of Bible versions. For many years he distributed thousands of books from a collection of over 100 different titles in support of the KJV position. Here he shares what he has come to see that has caused him to completely abandon his former position. – 254 pages, PB.

Salvation Of ALL, The: Creation's Final Destination
(A Biblical Look at Universal Reconciliation)

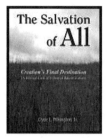

(#7001) The Gospel of our Lord and Savior, Jesus Christ is truly better "Good News" than we could ever have imagined. It is far more glorious than religion would ever have us believe. The Salvation of All is a book about a "Good News" that will reach its final goal in the salvation of all mankind. – 262 pages, PB.

Suffering: God's Forgotten Gift

Two gifts given to the believer are mentioned by Paul in Philippians 1:29. The first is *"to believe on Him."* This is a glorious gift. Every believer has been given this gift from God. Those who possess it may not even fully recognize it as a gift from Him, but indeed faith is God's wonderful gift to us. Faith is a rich gift from God, but there is also another gift from God to the believer mentioned by Paul in Philippians 1:29 that is equally as glorious. The second gift is *"also to suf-*

fer for His sake." This, too, is a glorious gift. Every believer has been given this gift from God as well, but those who possess it often do not fully recognize it for what it is. Indeed, suffering for His sake similarly is God's wonderful gift to us. Paul teaches us to embrace this second gift as well as we do the first! – 100 pages PB.

TO ORDER:

visit: ***ClydePilkington.com***
or call Toll Free: 1-800-784-6010